They took a Stand

GOD'S DETERMINED PEOPLE

BRIAN BLANDFORD

Illustrated by Ted Killian

Regal Books
A Division of GL Publications
Ventura, California, U.S.A.

Published by Regal Books
A Division of GL Publications
Ventura, California 93006
Printed in the U.S.A.

Scripture taken from the *Authorized King James Version*, Holy Bible.

The author and publisher have sought to locate and secure permission to reprint copyrighted materials in this manual. If any such acknowledgments have been omitted, the publisher would appreciate receiving the information so that proper credit may be given in future printings.

Library of Congress Cataloging-in-Publication Data

Blandford, Brian, 1937-
    They took a stand.

    Bibliography: p.
    1. Christian biography.   I. Title.
BR1700.2.B57   1986   270'.092'2   [B]   86-13878
ISBN 0-8307-1127-9

2 3 4 5 6 7 8 9 / 91 90 89 88

Rights for publishing this book in other languages are contracted by Gospel Literature International (GLINT) foundation. GLINT also provides technical help for the adaptation, translation, and publishing of Bible study resources and books in scores of languages worldwide. For further information, contact GLINT, Post Office Box 488, Rosemead, California, 91770, U.S.A., or the publisher.

Contents

Acknowledgments

Thanks—

As always, there are many people who have helped bring this book to birth:

> **my wife Mair,** and **our sons,** who put up with the inconveniences of an author in the house;
> **my father-in-law, Rev. Glyndwr Davies,** whose library was once again such a boon, and **my mother-in-law, Mrs. Mary Davies,** who soothed my brow for a week at the height of the writing fever;

my church, Central Baptist, Southampton, for allowing me time to complete the project;

Keith Phillips and others from the **Knowle West Fellowship** for giving me valuable material for the chapter on Cecil Phillips;

the biographers from whose work I've heavily drawn; my debt to them is immense. It would have been impossible in a book of this sort to have done the research into primary sources that true biography necessitates. I hope this book stimulates readers to go to the books listed at the end of each chapter, which will, to some degree, repay my debt. I also hope all direct quotations are duly acknowledged and no copyright infringements have occurred—any omissions will gladly be rectified.

Finally, my thanks to God for all the fine lives that provide the subject matter of these pages. To get to know these remarkable and challenging people has been a privilege. May they inspire others as they have inspired me.

Introduction

Here's a word to ponder: *anadromous.* Could be useful for Scrabble. Or, who knows? It might come up next time you play Trivial Pursuit. But it's not much of a game for the creatures it describes. They are the fish who live most of their lives in the oceans, but when the time comes to spawn, swim hundreds of miles up rivers to their breeding grounds.

Take the salmon. From goodness knows where in the Atlantic it will find its unerring way to a Scottish river mouth, and then the real battle begins. With incredible skill, tenacity, and strength, driven on by its instincts, it will fight its way yard by yard upstream against fast-flowing currents, making Olympic jumps up waterfalls, until it eventually arrives in the highlands, its strength all but spent. Sadly, many never do make it.

Is it worth it? That's something of a meaningless question. To swim against the stream is the only way the species can survive. It cannot run from the challenge. Choice is not something anadromous fish know anything about.

God needs anadromous men and women. People who will swim against the stream of selfishness and the current of conformity; those who will leap the waterfalls of worldliness and struggle through the blinding spray of falsehood. People who can never be content with the quiet millpond of bland spiritual mediocrity.

The men and women in this book are such people. They are a mixed bunch from different centuries and different countries; they are different in gifts—from a parlormaid who never passed a school examination in her life, to a man who spent his time teaching at the two greatest universities in Britain. But they all share a commitment to Christ that drove them to go against the stream, whatever the cost. In other words, they took a stand.

1

Martin Luther

It only took a few ferocious hammer blows from the stocky, cowled figure to send the nail deep into the heavy church door. The monk stood back from the long piece of paper as it curled and bobbed gently up and down, recovering from the violent banging. His eye roved with satisfaction over odd phrases here and there in the 95 little paragraphs arranged as though they were the monastery laundry list.

"Let's see what they make of *that!*" he thought as he hurried away.

It did not seem to him a hugely unusual event. He had simply, in his capacity as Doctor of Theology in the University of Wittenberg, Germany, announced his intention to debate some points he felt strongly about. A loyal son of the Holy Catholic Church, it was his duty, he felt, to point out where it was falling short of its ideals 1,517 years on from the birth of its founder. If only the Pope over there in Rome knew the true situation, he surely would agree. Greed and superstition were combining to make a mockery of the true Christian faith. Still, this debate would be a start. Those 95 statements on the church door would surely make *some* people aware.

So reasoned the insignificant monk from the insignificant little town about his not very significant action. But hardly had that laundry list of theological propositions stopped moving in the breeze then it blew in a hurricane that was to send the whole of Christendom turning cartwheels. Long accepted Church traditions had been questioned. The world would never be the same again.

Martin Luther was born on November 10, 1483, the son of Hans and Margaretta Luther, and baptized the next day, Saint Martin's Day.

"I do not remember this, but I believe my parents and fellow countrymen,"[1] was his later droll comment.

His father was not rich but had made something of a go of mining and owned foundries. He attributed this limited prosperity to Saint Anne, patron saint of miners. Young Martin was therefore able to have an education above what could usually be expected in those days. His parents had high hopes that a university training would be followed by a profitable law career that would see them comfortably off in their old age.

However, while their brilliant son was still in the process of gathering the precious degrees at Erfurt University, a terrifying experience changed his life's direction totally.

One sultry July night, the 21-year-old student was trudging across the open fields back to his university. He felt the air around him becoming semiliquid in its sticky thickness. The sky got darker and darker as the clouds piled on top of one another in swabs of dirty gray. Anxiously, the young man saw flashes on the horizon and heard distant rumbles. He hurried his step as the first heavy blobs splattered on his hood. He broke into a run as the rapidly accelerating rain drilled down with frightening force. Now the gap between lightning and thunderclap was so close that the storm must be almost overhead. Suddenly, Martin was hurled to the ground as though a giant had jumped on him. Breathless and almost senseless, he lay there moaning in terror. Surely this was God unleashing His terrible judgment on him. His medieval mind could think of no other explanation for the lightning bolt that had found him with the accuracy of a twentieth-century guided missile. This was it! He was on his way to hell! Instinctively, he cried out to his father's favorite saint, "Saint Anne, help me—and I will become a monk."

The rain still drumming down, though the storm was moving rapidly on, Martin looked at his soaking wet cloak, he studied his hands, he looked at the wet ground. He was still here on earth! He had survived! He scrambled up and made his wet, bedraggled way to his destination.

Martin assumed that it was Saint Anne who saved him. He kept his vow, to the chagrin—indeed, the outright anger—of his parents, especially his father, who could see his dreams of a plush retirement fading fast behind the traditional monastic vows of poverty, chastity and obedience. The resentment of Martin's parents was not helped by the fact he did not tell them of his decision until he was inside Erfurt monastery walls two weeks and one farewell party after the thunderstorm.

The first year went well. Martin seemed to have found his destiny. But it did not last. Temptation, sin, and fear of God's judgment could not be shut outside a monastery wall simply by slamming the door and sliding the bolt. The holiness of God became to him a fearsome thing, and this crystallized into a second spiritual crisis when he celebrated his first mass.

Not all monks became priests, but Martin's progress was such that he was selected. In the presence of his father, who had temporarily overcome his smoldering resentment to attend the momentous occasion, Martin stood at the holy altar. The air was heavy with incense; the other-worldly chanting of the monks echoed around the stone walls, heightening the sense of the mysterious. The nervous first-timer recited the solemn words with increasing awareness of God's might and purity. As he came to the words, "We offer unto Thee, the living, the true, the eternal God," he was, he said later, "utterly stupefied and terror-stricken." He could barely finish the service. What should have been his sunniest of days was overshadowed by a gloomy cloud as dark as that which had sent him to the monastery.

Afterwards, supper with his father was a miserable affair. The conversation was stilted and awkward. At last Luther senior erupted in bitterness.

"Just suppose, my son Martin, that it might have been an apparition of the Devil that led you into this life shut off from the world." Martin tried not to think too hard about that, but he knew that doubt was in his heart, too.

This incident increased Luther's determination. He wanted only two things: to serve Christ and to pass Judgment Day safely. The trouble was, the church in Martin's time taught that Jesus was a terrible unapproachable person, with standards that were impossible to keep. The Lord was portrayed to be like a teacher who sets 101 percent to be a passing grade. So the prospect of graduating at Judgment Day seemed too remote to have any hope. And the penalty of failing was too horrible to contemplate. The young Martin was haunted by the prospect of endless torment in hell. So he tried, and no one could have tried harder. He fasted, he prayed; he did without blankets and froze; he wearied his spiritual counselor, the saintly John Staupitz, with his continual coming to confess tiny sins that didn't seem to Staupitz sins at all.

"If ever a monk got to heaven by his monkery it was I . . . . If I had kept on any longer, I should have killed myself," Luther later explained.[2]

But it was no use. The barreness of all this activity came home to him when in 1510 he had a golden opportunity to go to the very center of sixteenth century Christianity—Rome. He went as a representative of his monastery, and there, ignoring the usual tourist attractions of the Eternal City, went to get closer to God. Instead, he was sickened by the worldliness of the church and the downright unbelieving flippancy of the clergy. He was also disappointed at what he thought would be a great spiritual experience. A flight of stairs was claimed to be from the house of Pontius Pilate. If a pilgrim climbed them on his knees, kissing each one and repeating the Pater Noster (the Latin Lord's Prayer) it was supposed to deliver a soul from purgatory (in the Catholic tradition, purgatory was a temporary place of punishment where saved but imperfect souls were purified before they entered heaven). When Martin got to the top, doubt overtook him, and from knees rubbed raw, he cried out, "Who knows whether it is so?"

So it was an increasingly unhappy Luther, uncertain of his faith, uncertain of his salvation, who returned to Germany. But he had a promotion which brought him into close contact with the one thing that could give him the answers—the Bible.

He was given his Doctor of Theology degree and appointed Professor of Bible at the new University of Wittenberg. Luther was already acquainted with the Bible and was fascinated by it, but in the church of those days the Bible was regarded as a somewhat dangerous thing to give it *too* much exposure. Reading it might expose the vast difference between God's plan for the church and what it had become.

Dr. Luther threw himself into his new job. He prepared lectures on Genesis, then on the Psalms. By 1515 he was teaching his students from Paul's letter to the Romans. Those studies were to be the great turning point of his life. The change was not immediate. The truth took time to dawn. In fact, he didn't feel he had full understanding until he went back to lecturing on the Psalms in 1519. But the materials that formed the robust later teaching on how a man is saved were all there for those first fortunate students to hear. You can't read Luther's joyous testimony without being thrilled along with him.

"I greatly longed to understand Paul's epistle to the Romans, and nothing stood in the way but that one expression, 'the justice of God,' because I took it to mean that justice whereby God is just and deals justly with punishing the unjust . . . though an impeccable monk, I stood before God as a sinner troubled in conscience, . . . therefore I did not love a just and angry God, but rather hated and murmured against him . . . . Night and day I pondered, until I saw the connection between the justice of God and the statement that 'the just shall live by faith' (Rom. 1:17). Then I grasped that the justice of God is that righteousness by which through grace and sheer mercy God justifies us through faith. Thereupon I felt myself to be reborn and to have gone through open doors to paradise."[3]

Martin's greatest joy was to discover that God loved him, and that he could love God. Paradise indeed!

Along with his life-giving discovery came an increasing discontent, bordering on anger, at the way the church portrayed to the people the way of salvation. It was all "works" and not grace. Heaven had to be earned by effort, not gratefully received as a gift. But worse, and totally horrible to the reborn Luther, salvation was actually being sold in the form of indulgences.

The theory behind the sharp commercialism was this:

Most people lived lives far, far below the standard God required. Therefore, when they died, even though they believed in Christ they were not fit to go straight to heaven, and must instead go to purgatory, where their sins would be purged in painful fire until at last they qualified for the bliss of heaven. The process could take many centuries, depending on the degree of guilt that had to be erased. However, there were a few very good people, the "Saints," who not only lived up to the standard, but went beyond it, and so had surplus goodness to spare. Preeminently, Christ had lived a life of absolute perfection. So all this goodness of Christ and the saints accumulated in a treasury of merit, and the Pope had the authority to dispense "indulgences" from this treasury to deserving people. So the church in Martin Luther's day cheapened the sacrifice Jesus paid on the cross by teaching that forgiveness of sins could be bought or earned. Grieving relatives believed that certain prescribed acts could release their dead loved ones from part or all of their sentence in purgatory. Originally, the indulgences were granted in return for some noble service, such as taking part in a crusade, but over the years it had become more and more debased until they were granted for such things as seeing or touching the bones of a saint or some other supposed holy relic—and such a viewing or touching carried a fee. It was your opportunity to buy your relatives out of purgatory.

Luther became increasingly disturbed for two reasons: one was that the patron of his own University of Wittenberg, Elector Frederick the Wise, was particularly proud of his collection of relics, (bone fragments, pieces of cloth, or other objects which were said to have belonged to Christ or specific saints). Frederick loved to show off his relics as an art connoisseur might show people his paintings. The second was the appearance in the vicinity of a Dominican friar named Tetzel who was there at the express command of the Pope to raise money to build the new Saint Peter's basilica in Rome.

Even in those days such massive construction projects did not come cheap, so what better and quicker way to raise the cash than this happy trade that would not only pay for the Sistine Chapel dome, but would also supposedly send countless grandpas and grandmas into heaven?

Tetzel was a good salesman, who could today have made himself a millionaire from a used car lot in no time. He would arrive at a town preceded by a cross with the papal arms, and the Pope's Bull (official letter) of Indulgence born on a cushion. He would then make a tear-jerking speech.

"Listen to the voices of your dear dead relatives and friends, beseeching you and saying, 'Pity us, pity us. We are in dire torment from which you can redeem us for a pittance' .... Hear the father saying to his son, the mother to her daughter, 'We bore you, nourished you ... and you are so cruel and hard that now you are not willing for so little to set us free.'"[4]

That was some load of moral pressure to bear! To clinch his sale, Tetzel even had a commercial jingle:

> *As soon as the coin falls into the chest*
> *A soul flies from purgatory into rest.*

It was a winner. The money rolled in, and bargain hunters came home to Wittenberg happily waving their bits of paper assuring them of their trophies from the Pearly Gates sales.

Luther could stand it no longer. And so on All Saints Eve, October 31, 1517, with his ruler Frederick about to make his annual exhibition of relics with its associated sale of indulgences, the twin sources of his irritation provoked Luther to the door-nailing episode we began with. Up went his "95 Theses," or propositions for debate. They contained such statements as: "The Pope has neither the will nor the power to remit any penalties beyond those he himself has imposed .... The Pope can remit no guilt.... Hence those preachers of indulgences are wrong when they say that a man is absolved and saved from every penalty by the Pope's indulgences."⁵

The idea was a flop. Or so it seemed. Not a single fellow-academic took up the challenge and debated with Luther. But there was something mightier than a closed university debating chamber that took a hand, and that was the printing press. Luther never intended his propositions should be translated into German from his Latin and sent all over Germany, but they were, and totally unexpectedly they seemed to be just what the country was waiting for. It seemed a lot of people found Luther articulated just what they had been wanting to say; people like Erasmus of Rotterdam, who had seen the abuses of the Roman church with enormous clarity, and wrote with courage against them.

In addition to this unsought publicity, Luther rather naively sent a copy to Bishop Albert of Mainz, whose name was on the instructions given to Tetzel. Albert sent a copy to the Pope himself.

The result was that the debate grew larger and larger. It was not long before Luther was being summoned to appear in Rome to answer charges of heresy. Not at all willing to go, Martin appealed to his patron, the Elector Frederick. An involved series of negotiations went on through the court chaplain Spalatin, who turned out to a be good friend, that led to Luther receiving a personal hearing at Augsberg with the papal legate, Cardinal Cajetan. Cajetan's job was to act as a sort of official ambassador for the pope. His instructions were to get Martin Luther to retract the controversial ideas he had been stating or to bring him bound to Rome. Luther frankly refused to recant. For three days he argued, and the meeting degenerated into a shouting match. Along the way, his old spiritual adviser Staupitz released Luther from his monastic vows. This meant that Luther was no longer a priest. He was greatly hurt for he still wanted to reform the church from within. Then Luther got wind of the plans to deliver him bound to Rome, so he made a hasty escape, riding like the wind without breeches, spurs, stirrup, or sword.

Back in Wittenberg, he realized his security was no stronger than tissue paper. He did not know how Frederick would react. Would the ruler have him delivered to Rome? After all, the Elector must be feeling sore about the attack on relics, given his great enthusiasm for them. He had taken ages to build up his unique collection which included (if you can believe it) a "genuine" thorn from the crown, guaranteed to have pierced Christ's brow. Luther prepared himself for the worst. He knew the pressure was on Frederick from Rome, and for a conscientious Christian prince to say no was almost too much to hope. But amazingly, Frederick did say no, and told Cajetan by letter that he saw no reason why his university professor should revoke what he said. Instead, let him be given the opportunity to debate in the universities as he wanted to.

Luther read the reply almost ecstatically, "Good God, with what joy I read them and read them over again!"[6]

Martin Luther now had a following in Wittenberg almost like a fan club. His teaching was popular with his students, and fellow teachers such as Philip Melanchthon and Andrew Carlistadt soaked up his words. Outside of Wittenberg, interest grew still more, and the reformer's desire for a university debate came to pass when Duke George invited him to Leipzig to dispute with one of the Roman church's top debaters, John Eck, professor at the University of Ingolstadt.

The occasion was like the American Superbowl, or the English Cup Final, with each of the disputants arriving with his army of supporters. There were 200 students armed with battle-axes accompanying Luther, and the crowd who wanted to witness the contest was so great that the event had to be transferred to the great auditorium of the Duke's Castle. For 10 days in that 1519 summer the verbal battle raged. With no ringside judge to pronounce a verdict it is an open question who won. But one important admission Eck wrung out of Luther made the Wittenberg champion look at his position in a new way. The admission was that Luther agreed with the teachings of John Huss. That was a bit frightening—Huss had been burned as a heretic years before. Now as Luther saw that he was closer and closer to what Huss believed and taught (and Hussites saw it too, writing to encourage Luther) he found the future path getting farther and farther from his original ideal of reforming Rome from within. As for Eck, it was with triumphant satisfaction that he reported personally to the Pope that Luther was "the Saxon Huss."

A year later just how far he had moved along that different path became clear when he published an astounding tract that almost sent the new Saint Peter's dome tumbling on the Pope's head in shock. Called *The Babylonian Captivity,* it cut the seven Catholic sacraments to two—baptism and communion, and took from the latter the priestly control that Luther now believed to be unscriptural. The church taught that the communion was effective regardless of the spirituality of the people taking part, provided it was celebrated by a valid priest. Luther said no; the person who receives the sacrament must have faith for there to be any benefit to him. Otherwise, the rite was no better than superstition or magic.

But greater "heresy" was to come. The outrageous Martin denied that the priest "makes God" when he held up the wafer to heaven. For centuries the church had taught that when the priest "elevated the host" and said in Latin, "This is my body," the bread actually changed into the body of Christ. The power of the priesthood lay to a large degree in their exclusive claim to work this miracle.

The Babylonian Captivity sent shock waves rippling through the church. From his hunting lodge the Pope had already issued one of the famous documents of history, the Bull known by its first Latin words *Exsurge Domine* (Arise O Lord) which gave Luther 60 days to retract his statements or else be excommunicated (denied membership in the church). It demanded too the burning of his books. When the Bull eventually reached Luther himself after some considerable delay, far from contritely conforming to its call for submission, he was furious. There was a bonfire all right. At the invitation of Melancthon, all the students gathered to have a fine old time sending up in smoke books of church law and scholastic theology plus the works of Eck and Luther's other opponents. Luther personally threw on the papal bull and watched with satisfaction as the lead seal melted in the flames. The celebration ended with the students going around Wittenberg in a cart with another bull speared on a pole, and an indulgence on the point of a sword. As they went they sang the *Te Deum,* a hymn of praise.

Officially excommunicated he might be, but Luther was not going to give in without a fight. Fortunately for him, Frederick, though claiming neutrality, was sticking by him. Also, the German nation was feeling a certain amount of glee at the way their incorrigible son was taking on the Italians. Religious considerations they might not understand, but national pride they did. So it was that largely through Frederick's efforts, Luther was given one last chance to defend himself. This was to be before the Holy Roman Emperor, Charles V, who, though largely a figurehead ruler, carried immense prestige. The occasion was to be the next meeting (called a Diet) of the rulers of Germany, the place, Worms, on the Rhine River. There were several hiccups before it took place, with the invitation being given, withdrawn, then offered again. But at last, the decisive confrontation took place that would decide the course of church history from then until our own day.

Some of Luther's friends would have stopped him going for his own sake. But once the reformer had set his mind to go there was no turning back. He would go, he affirmed, though there were as many devils as tiles on the roofs.

April 16, 1521, Worms.

A beautiful spring day. The town has so many people in it they are falling over one another. The inns are full, and every spare room from castle to peasant's hovel is taken.

At around noon the word spreads rapidly that Luther is drawing near and the crowd, probably about 2,000 strong, congregates around the city gate. It seems like a state occasion, and sure enough, there is the imperial herald in uniform waiting for the No. 1 celebrity. But when the puffs of dust on the horizon take a more solid shape, it becomes almost ludicrous. For here is no golden coach, but a rough Saxon two-wheel cart, lumbering and jolting its handful of occupants mercilessly through the ruts and stones. Nevertheless, excited and cheering, the crowd follows in a disorganized procession as the herald solemnly fulfills his duty and conducts Martin and his friends to their lodging. The hero of the hour has had a long and tiring journey and is glad for the 24 hours respite.

The next afternoon the herald calls again, keeping time and route secret from the crowd, and within minutes Luther stands before his Emperor, Charles V. Sitting around the room are the various electors (German princes), and his theological opponent, Archbishop Eck of Trier (a different Eck than the one at Leipzig). He has a proven track record of effective opposition to the heretic. When he held a Luther book-burning it was so thorough that not one book could be found afterwards.

Emperor and Luther eye each other.

"That man will never make a heretic of me!"[7] snaps Charles testily. He seems to be regretting that he allowed himself to be talked into this event.

The archbishop stands and opens his questioning.

"Martin Luther, the Emperor and the realm have summoned you hither, that you may say and tell them whether you have composed these books and others which bear your name, and, secondly, that you may let us know whether you propose to defend and stand by these books."[8] Eck laboriously recites 25 titles from the pile of books in front of him. Martin listens, his impatience growing. He knows what he will reply before the first title is off the Archbishop's lips: "The books are all mine, and I have written more."

Eck speaks again. "Do you defend them all, or do you reject a part?"

This time Martin hesitates. He draws his cheeks in and frowns from indecision. At last he answers. "This touches God and His Word. This affects the salvation of souls . . . . I beg you. Give me time to think it over."[9]

Now it is Eck's turn to furrow his brow. He is amazed and somewhat mocking.

"Are you a professor of theology, and must you have time to know whether you agree with your own books or not?"

A consultation follows with the emperor. After a long time the worried Martin hears the decision concerning his request.

"Martin Luther, we are surprised you do not have your answer ready, in that you knew why you were coming. We are under no obligation to grant your request for a respite. Nevertheless, from our pure grace and mercy, you may have until four o'clock tomorrow. But be warned: we strictly admonish you to use the time well. We expect a change of attitude when next you stand here."

Martin shuffles away, downcast. He has bought himself time, but is it any good? Some inside the hall and those who hear the news outside are baffled. Is Martin losing his nerve? Is he on the point of retracting his statements, at least in part, after all? Where is the fearless writer who exposed false doctrines taught by the Church? Is this really he?

The whole of Worms goes to bed that night wondering. They are living through a cliff-hanger, and no one can tell how it will end. As for the beleagured doctor, he is in his lodgings wondering, writing, and praying. The outcome is a series of concise notes that will provide the basis for his defense the next day.

The next day comes, and at four Martin is once again conducted by the herald to the castle. This time they are in a larger auditorium, for the whole Diet is in session, and no one wants to miss what is going on.

Eck stands and makes a disparaging oration rebuking Luther for his dallying and repeating the questions with a demand for clear answers.

Luther's voice as he begins betrays none of the uncertainty of the previous night. It is clear, moderate, and firm. The audience hangs on his every word as he reaffirms his acknowledgment of the books. Then as to whether he upholds them all, he divides them into different classes. Some, he says, even the infamous official letter from the Pope accepted as true; he cannot retract those. Others were arguments against the papacy. Eck leans forward intently. Luther continues without so much as a blink.

"Yet the canon law of the papists itself says the papal laws and doctrines that differ from the gospel or what the fathers teach should be counted thrown out as error. If then, I take back these books, all I shall do is add weight to tyranny."

Every word is weighed by the audience. Martin seems to be putting a noose around his neck. But there is more. He defines a third class of books, those that had attacked the defenders of the papacy. Of these, he says, he does regret the overstrong language that is not really in place, but then, he does not profess to be a saint.

"Yet I can't retract even these writings, for then I should be sanctioning the reign of tyranny and wickedness."

The audacity of his reply almost takes the breath of the

archbishop away. But militant Martin is not finished yet. He makes one concession: let the Emperor, or anyone at all from highest to lowest show him from Scripture that he is wrong and he will be the first to hurl his books into the fire.

Eck draws himself up to his full height, takes a deep breath, and makes his reply.

"Your plea to be heard from Scripture is what heretics always do. You have no right to call into question the most holy, orthodox faith. I demand of you, Martin—give me a frank answer without ifs—do you or do you not repudiate your books and all their errors?"

Everyone is eager to hear what must be Luther's final unequivocal response. With emotion in his voice, but without any uncertainty, he speaks.

"Since then Your Majesty and your Lordships desire a straightforward answer, I'll give you one, without 'ifs'; and without 'buts.' Unless I am convicted by Scripture and plain reason—I do not accept the authority of popes and councils for they have often contradicted each other—my conscience is captive to the Word of God. I cannot and I will not recant anything, for to go against conscience is neither right nor safe. Here I stand. I can do no other. So help me, God. Amen."[10]

The emotion of the moment has almost overcome him, but he repeats his declaration in Latin as he is required to do, and then withdraws as quickly as he can to his lodging, drained and limp, leaving the assembly, the emperor, and the archbishop to make of it what they will.

The inevitable result was that the official assembly issued an edict condemning Luther. He set out to return to Wittenberg with a companion wondering how much longer he could survive. With church and state against him, he did not think it could be long. But there were surprises in store.

The first was that as their cart trundled toward the wood at Eisenach, they were suddenly set upon by an armed gang. There was a great deal of banging about and noise, and Luther's companion was able to make off, while Luther himself was captured, put on a horse, and then led on a route that twisted, turned back on itself, and seemed to go on forever. A day went by like this, with Luther more and more baffled and confused as to what was happening. Then as the sun dipped down to the horizon, the dark, gigantic shape of a castle seemed to fill the reddening sky. Martin found himself being led towards the huge oak doors which were swung open to meet him, and he was pushed through, and heard them slam shut behind. Then suddenly, the atmosphere was changed. There was laughing, and joking, and back-slapping. The amazed Martin found the whole thing had been an elaborate plot to bring him to safety at Wartburg Castle for as long as was necessary. It had all been planned by Elector Frederick, who was now firmly on Luther's side. The Wartburg Castle was virtually unoccupied, but even so in the unlikely event of Martin's whereabouts being discovered, it would be unlikely to be captured. It was virtually impregnable.

Luther wrote to Spalatin from his new home: "Here I was stripped of my own clothes and clad in those of a knight. I am letting my hair and my beard grow, and you would hardly know me—indeed for some time I have hardly known myself!"

Not that Luther was especially pleased to be shut up as he was. But he used the time well, and during the coming year he wrote ceaselessly, and made one of the most lasting and far-reaching of all his contributions to German life: he translated the New Testament into his mother tongue. Future years would see him translate the Old Testament as well. The impact of this work can only be fully comprehended when one realizes that in Luther's day most Bibles were written in Latin and could not be read by ordinary people. Now the

Scriptures on which Martin based his electrifying teaching could be made available to German-speaking people.

Luther could not keep away from Wittenberg forever, and eventually he risked going back. His popularity was such that the Pope never dared to capture him. Martin was able to push forward the reforms at Wittenberg, though sometimes he found himself having to hold back the more zealous of his followers, who "out-Luthered" Luther.

One radical change Luther certainly approved of was the liberation of Christian ministry from the restriction of celibacy—though he had no idea what dynamite effect the move was going to have on his own life. As monks left their monasteries and nuns left their nunneries, so he began to act as a sort of marriage broker. The trouble was he had one nun left over: Katherine von Bora. After two years, there seemed no other answer but that he should marry her himself. It was not perhaps the most romantic way to approach marriage, but in fact it proved to be an ideal match, and the warm happiness of domestic life, the joy of children, blessings he had never dreamed of experiencing, were Martin's. His table always had a troop of people around it. His children and also his students hung on his every pronouncement, noting them down as "table talk." The Luther household became the pattern for parsonage life in the protestant church to this very day.

The years that followed Worms were as eventful as those that came before it, with crises along with triumphs. The extraodinary life of Martin Luther cannot be told in one chapter. You must go to the rich store of the biography named at the end. Our story ends where it began, at the same church door that bore witness under the monk's hammer blows to Luther's determination to see God's truth vindicated. Now, in February 1546, the door is open and through its archway there moves a solemn procession bearing a coffin. Martin Luther, the monk who took his stand, is dead. But there is not one person present who doubts that his spirit lives on.

For further reading: *Here I Stand* by Roland Bainton (Mentor Books)

Notes
1. E.G. Rupp and B. Drewery *Documents of Modern History: Martin Luther* (London: Edward Arnold), p. 1.
2. R.H. Bainton, *Here I Stand* (Tennessee: Abingdon Press, 1950)p. 34.
3. Bainton, *Here I Stand,* p. 49.
4. Bainton, *Here I Stand,* p. 59.
5. Rupp and Drewery, *Documents of Modern History: Martin Luther,* pp. 19-21.
6. Bainton, *Here I Stand,* p. 78.
7. Bainton, *Here I Stand,* p. 141.
8. Rupp and Drewery, *Documents of Modern History: Martin Luther* p. 56
9. Bainton, *Here I Stand,* p. 141.
10. Bainton, *Here I Stand,* p. 144.

2

Dwight L. Moody

It was getting near vacation time, and the weary teacher of the little community school in Northfield, Massachusetts, had a great idea for getting her unruly, impatient class of farm children over the last day of term. She would have a program of recitation before an audience of school committee, parents, and clergy. She smiled her professional smile of approval as one little lad held his hearers spellbound while he declaimed Mark Antony's speech lamenting Caesar's death. Dramatically, the young orator waved his hand toward the box he had brought to represent the emperor's coffin. Then, with a flourish, he lifted the lid. In a bound, "Caesar," a spitting fur-ball of a tomcat, was out of his coffin—to the audience's stunned surprise followed by their total collapse in laughter.

The impish speech-maker was Dwight L. Moody, destined to become the greatest evangelist of the nineteenth century. His sense of fun never left him, nor his ability to cut through a pompous occasion. His way with words that had held his school audience was to develop into a mastery of the art that would hold thousands enthralled. Those ingredients for his future career were there in that schoolhouse then, though there was a lot that had to happen before God could use them.

Dwight's family was desperately poor. Born February 5, 1837, he was only four when his father died, probably from too much drink, leaving his mother with six boys, a girl, and no money—for his father was bankrupt. The creditor came and took everything he could, including the furniture. It was all the boys could do to hide their father's tools from the heartless man. Only a compassionate law kept him from taking the house. And then next month, to add to Widow Moody's troubles she gave birth to twins.

The good lady came from that stern Puritan stock that had forged the New World in the seventeenth century. Against all odds she did a marvelous job raising her nine children. The only way she could cope was by putting her kids to work as soon as they were able to hold a hoe, which meant that education was spasmodic for Dwight. He never did learn to spell.

Widow Moody was pious, but did not know the gospel. The strong religion in Northfield was Unitarianism—a brand of belief descended from the Arianism you will read about in the chapter on Athanasius. It made for a troubling religion, without warmth.

By the time Dwight was 17, the freedom- and fun-loving Moody was longing to strike out on his own. And, with the new railroad opposite his home stretching enticingly away into the blue, he packed his bag and clambered on board the puffing monster to take himself away to Boston and fame and fortune—especially fortune. His mother and three older brothers strongly disapproved.

Dwight found a job with his Uncle Samuel Socrates Holton (who was none too willing). He wrote home: "I have a room up in the third story and I can open my winder and there is 3 grat buildings full of girls the hansomest thare is in the city and they will sware like parrets." Well, we said he never learned to spell.

With his broad shoulders in a thick-set five-foot-ten frame, his firm muscles and his head set down on his chest with hardly any neck to separate the two, he was a strong youth. He could take care of himself with his fists if he needed. But one stronger than he was about to lay hold of him.

Uncle Socrates, as a condition of employment, made DL (he preferred to be called by his initials or surname rather than "Dwight") promise to attend Mount Vernon Church and Sunday School (Congregationalist). His Sunday School teacher was Edward Kimball, who welcomed him and saw he was not embarrassed in front of the other boys by his lack of Bible knowledge.

Moody fell asleep during the first sermon in church, but the minister, Dr. E. N. Kirk, was to hold his attention in the coming months as DL heard the gospel for the first time. DL tried to put off decision: "I thought I would wait until I died and then become a Christian."[1] Meanwhile, he was fast becoming Socrates' best salesman.

Kimball decided in the midst of a revival to speak to Moody about Christ. With something of a quaking heart, he went to the shoe store. "I went up to him and put my hand on his shoulder, and as I leaned over I placed my foot upon a shoebox. I asked him to come to Christ who loved him and who wanted his love and should have it." And Moody did, though Kimball thought he had made a poor job of presenting the gospel claim to him. Moody went outside into the Boston springtime and "fell in love with everything. I never loved the bright sun shining over the earth so much before. And when I heard the birds singing their sweet songs, I fell in love with the birds. Everything was different."[2]

Next morning, DL went to church still thinking "the old sun shone a good deal brighter than it ever had before."

From the very beginning DL was no secret disciple. He went straight back to Northfield for a few days to try to win his family to Christ, but with no success.

He was not much more successful in his application for church membership. Asked by the interviewing deacons, "What has Christ done for us all?" his tongue-tied answer was, "I don't know. I think Christ has done a great deal for us. But I don't think of anything particular as I know of." It was another year before DL persuaded the deacons that he understood enough of the gospel to warrant membership—and even then it was touch and go. Yet he would later be the man who helped hundreds of thousands to know clearly and simply what makes a man a Christian.

Just as there was no doubt about his zeal for Christ, there was no doubt about his zest for business and his ability to sell shoes. He felt he had outgrown Boston; he determined to go West like so many other young men in those robust, exciting, pioneering days when everything seemed possible to go-getters with guts. So despite family opposition, he arrived in Chicago September 18, 1856, and got a job with Wiswall's Shoe Store. So good was DL that he was put in charge of meeting the constant immigrant trains arriving at the depot to badger the Windy City's bewildered new arrivals to buy his wares. Moody's aim was to get rich quick in this fortune-hungry place. "I used to pray to God to give me $100,000," he said, and he wrote home, "I can make money faster here than I can in Boston."[3] Astute business deals in land increased his prospect of a rich future. He saw no conflict between his material ambitions and his enjoyment of religion (an enjoyment not marred by Uncle Calvin, who silenced him at the prayer meetings because of his uncouth grammar). He developed a taste for sermons, and would hear as many as he could. It was while sampling the fare at First Baptist that he spied a 13-year-old girl named Emma. Her face imprinted itself on his memory.

Back in his own church, Plymouth Congregational, DL turned his business success to good account. During special meetings, he rented (such was the custom of those days) four pews and filled them nightly with customers, or even passersby from the streets.

The same initiative and drive showed even clearer later that year, when Moody decided to help out at a mission Sunday School. The superintendent said that he had 12 teachers already, with only 16 children to teach. But if DL could raise a class himself, then fine. Moody went on a round-up operation the next Sunday that brought 18 of the roughest, wildest, dirtiest Chicago street urchins. Then instead of teaching them, he handed over the gang to the unemployed teachers and went off to get more "clients." He went on doing this until the school was overflowing, and new teachers were having to be recruited. His heart missed a couple of beats when one week he saw that one of the new teachers was the girl he had seen in First Baptist—Emma—now 15 and looking mighty pretty. Never a procrastinator, he quickly got himself introduced, and met her father, Fleming H. Revell.

Business was going well too. He had gone on to another firm, C.H. Henderson, and quickly made his mark as their debt collector. The only problem was the job involved traveling a lot, and he found when he was away, his Sunday School gang drifted. He became concerned about the inability of the traditional Sunday Schools to meet the needs of the poor and underprivileged. With the help of a couple of friends, he got hold of his original bunch of ruffians who were led by a tough youngster called Jimmy Sexton, and invited them to start a new Sunday School.

Their first meeting place was an old, abandoned freight car. When that got too small, they rented a one-and-a-half story saloon. Then that became overcrowded, and they took on the North Market hall, which had to be cleaned up from the previous night's dance every week. DL got up at six every Sunday morning to do it, being unwilling to employ labor on the Sabbath, he regarded sweeping the floors as true a work for God as leading the service.

The numbers rose to 600. The meetings were riotous. Moody believed the best way to keep interest was not to have anything too long, so there would be singing, a short talk, more singing, another short talk, and so on.

DL was still not teaching the children; he was painfully conscious of his lack of education. Eventually he did begin speaking at evening meetings. But even then he was thrown into a state of confusion if he learned a minister was present. Personal witness was another matter, however. He was fearless in talking to anyone about Christ and their need of Him. It was to be a mark of his life, even when he became a famous mass evangelist. He made it a vow to never pass a day without speaking to someone about Christ.

Once, in 1860, DL was on a train and leaned across to his fellow passenger and asked, "Are you a Christian?" It so happened that the man was a banker, an important man. But in spite of his status, he was willing to listen, and right there in the carriage the banker knelt down to receive Christ as his Saviour. It was just one among many such incidents.

Not all welcomed the shock of Moody's challenge. He would cry in public at the rebuffs heaped upon him but made up his mind always to "keep sweet" when opposed. But one man who cursed and insulted him for so intruding on his personal business was found three months later on Moody's doorstep after midnight asking what he must do to be saved, confessing he had not been able to sleep since the evangelist addressed him so boldly.

Moody was now working for C.H. Henderson on a commission basis. And because he was so good at his job, he earned enough to free himself more and more for evangelistic and Sunday School work. He had moved away from his original goal simply to make a fortune; his intention now was to earn money to pay for philanthropic and Christian ventures; he had all the makings of a successful, generous-hearted, Christian businessman. But then in mid-1860 something happened that changed that worthy, neat scheme once and for all.

It started with one of his Sunday School teachers collapsing in Moody's office in great distress and obvious weakness. He just received the terrible news that he was terminally ill and must return home to New York. His distress was not, however, so much over the physician's diagnosis as the realization that he must leave his Sunday School class without ever having led a single one of them to become a true Christian.

"I really believe I have done the girls more harm than good," the man grieved.

Moody was astounded. He had never heard anyone talk with such concern about the salvation of children before. He agreed with the teacher to go to each of the girls' homes. After 10 days, all had been visited and everyone of them had asked Christ into her life. Moody suggested that they all meet together for a farewell dinner. After the meal, the teacher prayed for each girl, and then the girls, one after the other, prayed for him. Moody was totally astonished at the love and feeling that was there. It seemed to him like a piece of heaven had descended into the room. "O God," he prayed, "let me die rather than lose the blessing I have received tonight!"

The next evening they saw the teacher off from the depot—another very emotional experience that all but broke Moody up. It radically changed him.

"I didn't know what this was going to cost me. I was disqualified for business; it had become distasteful to me. I had a taste of another world, and cared no more for making money. For some days after, the greatest struggle of my life took place. Should I give up business and give myself wholly to Christian work, or should I not?"[4]

It took three months for this controversy with God to be settled. There was a lot to sort out. His ambitions for money had to be surrendered; his hopes of an early marriage to Emma (the two had been getting very close) might be dashed; the risks involved seemed enormous. But indecision was never one of Moody's faults. Like the Apostle Peter, who also gave up business for the Lord, when he moved, he moved wholeheartedly.

"God helped me to decide aright, and I have never regretted my choice."[5]

Autumn 1860 saw DL without paid employment, without lodgings, bedded down on a sofa at the YMCA like some hobo. He was determined to live as cheaply as he could on his savings so that he would have enough money to spend freely on his Sunday School. When the funds ran out, he felt the call of God had run out too, and would go back to business. Even when he was appointed a YMCA official, he refused to take a salary, and meanwhile spent recklessly on all kinds of good works such as providing physicians to the poor. Moody was never a "save-the-soul-and-forget-the-body" evangelist.

Now free to devote all his time to the Sunday School, Moody seemed to be everywhere, getting more and more kids to come. He would get them to stay, listen, and be converted. His methods were brash and shocking to some, and he got the nickname "Crazy Moody." No one dared stay away because he would be after them.

Once, DL visited a house to find the father absent and a jug of whiskey on the table. Taking the man's children in tow, as he marched out of the house Moody swept up the jug in his arms and poured the contents in the gutter outside, smashing the crock for good measure.

On the next visit, the father was there, and boy was he angry! He started to take his coat off, with threats hot enough to scorch the wallpaper. "Hold on a minute," the young evangelist cried. "If I am to be thrashed, let me pray for you all before you do it." He fell to his knees and prayed with earnestness which didn't need much working up. As he rose, the man said with some embarrassment, "You had better just take the kids, not a whipping"—which Moody was only too thankful to do.

On another occasion Moody waited three hours for a girl who had promised to come but let him down. Seeing her the next day, he chased her for block after block, finally wrestling her to the floor in a saloon. Eventually, the girl's whole family was converted. (Today they would probably have taken him to court for assault!)

Probably no man on earth has lived out more literally the command in the parable of Jesus, "Go out into the highways and hedges, and compel them to come in" (Luke 14:23, *KJV*). His friend in the work, John Farwell, gave him an Indian pony to help, as good a runabout as ever there was before VW Beetles. Scores of children found their way to Moody's Sunday School on its back, pony and children enticed on by the evangelist's endless supply of candies.

Not that Moody was soft. He showed his determination when he taught one persistent troublemaker a lesson. While he took the rough fellow to the basement, he instructed Farwell to get the school members to sing the loudest hymn they knew. When the hymn finished, Moody returned, flushed with exertion, the boy somewhat sore. A month later the lad was converted.

The school was becoming famous; even Abraham Lincoln visited it. But soon its carefree days were clouded by the darkest national event in the history of the United States—the Civil

War of 1861-65. DL would not fight himself because he could not bring himself to take up a gun against a fellow human being, but he vigorously supported Lincoln and the North, and recruited soldiers from the Sunday School. Jimmy Sexton, his original Chicago tough, eventually became a Colonel. DL was asked to provide religious ministrations at Camp Douglas. He began to have to overcome his reluctance to speak to a crowd of people of his own age. As the war went on, he was often ministering at the front. Moody made up his mind he would not let a man die without telling him of Christ and of heaven.

But the war was not all strain and tension. Wedding bells rang on August 28, 1862, for DL and Emma. It was a love-match, and Emma gave DL not only a domestic base to which he could retreat from his ceaseless public activity, but also smoothed down some of DL's rough edges with that gentle art only wives have the secret of.

Toward the end of the war, a new building opened in Illinois at a cost of $24,000. A sign announced: *Ever Welcome to This House of God Are Strangers and the Poor.* A song had the same message:

> Go bring him in, there is room to spare,
> Here are food and shelter and pity;
> And we'll not shut the door
> 'Gainst one of Christ's poor
> Though you bring every child in the city.[6]

And so now Moody had a church of his own. But he still did not count himself a preacher. Preachers for the new church were supplied by Chicago Theological Seminary. But one Sunday when a student failed to arrive, Farwell suggested Moody preach. From that time he preached every Sunday in the evening. The next stage in the making of Dwight L. Moody was complete.

Emma had asthma. But if anyone ever doubted that God uses sickness, what happened next—of crucial importance to Moody's life—should cause a change of opinion. The illness spurred DL to fulfill an ambition to visit England. He wanted especially to meet three heroes: George Williams, founder of the YMCA; George Müller of Bristol, the man who ran huge orphan homes, praying to God alone for funds; and C.H. Spurgeon, famous Baptist preacher of London. After a seasick crossing, DL said when he arrived, "I do not expect to visit this country again." In fact, the initial impressions the Moodys had of England were almost all negative, but over the next four months they melted somewhat under the warm appreciation shown them. DL met all three heroes, and in the process stimulated the London YMCA to start a noon prayer meeting like the one operating in Chicago.

The English soon got a taste of his daring but lovable humor when he spoke at the annual meeting of Sunday School Union. Asked to move a vote of thanks to Lord Shaftesbury, the great Christian social reformer, Moody said, "Now about this vote of thanks to the 'noble Earl.' I don't see why we should thank him any more than he should thank us." Lord Shaftesbury was delighted.

Moody was also invited to speak in Dublin, Ireland, where he met a boyish, insignificant man named Moorhouse who offered to preach for him in Chicago. Moody was totally unimpressed and took care not to let on when he was returning so that the man would not be encouraged to follow through with his offer.

Several weeks later Moorhouse turned up in Chicago. Moody groaned. Whatever was he to do with this Englishman who spoke funny? Perhaps dodging things a bit, he decided to let him have a trial while he was away. However, when he came back he found the people loved the man, and then when

Moody heard Moorhouse for himself he was completely won over. It was so odd. Night after night the baby-faced evangelist with the strange accent would preach on the same text— John 3:16—going through the Scriptures from Genesis to Revelation each time to show how much God loved men. Moody had never heard preaching like it before. It was odd. Every sermon was the same, and yet every sermon was different. And always, like a throbbing heartbeat, there was the theme of the love of God. Moody's own style had been very aggressive and full of blood and thunder. It began to be transformed under the Englishman's gentle influence. Years later, a great English minister testified of Moody, "He could never speak of a lost soul without tears of Christly compassion in his eyes." It was Moorhouse who opened those tear ducts. Moorhouse also taught Moody how to study the Bible systematically for the first time. God had brought another piece of the puzzle into place to make the complete evangelist.

Not that Moody was looking for a career as a preacher. He was still firmly a Chicago Sunday School leader, with responsibilities in that city ever mounting. There was the church, and his YMCA work there as well, and enough souls in the Windy City to keep him occupied for two lifetimes at least, even at his rate of work. Moody's energy seemed boundless. One New Year's day he made 200 calls on his flock!

But he did want to see his work move effectively, and though he was virtually tone-deaf, he believed music was the way. He decided he needed a songleader.

In July 1870, Moody attended the International Convention of the YMCA and met the 29-year-old Pennsylvania delegate, Ira D. Sankey. Once he had heard him sing, Moody gave Sankey the shock of the life. "You must give up your job and come to Chicago!" he told him.

Sankey, married with two children, swallowed hard. But

within six months Sankey was to proclaim that Moody had "prayed me out of business." There was first a trial week in 1871, and then Sankey set up in bachelor accommodations in the rebuilt YMCA with the option of going back to his home if things did not work out. They were a perfect complement to each other. Sankey—neat, exact, almost pompous, while Moody cut through all the established order of things with his glorious informality.

In spite of outward success, all was not well. Moody was experiencing a spiritual desert within, though not admitting it. The attendances of 1,200-1,800 would lift him, but did not satisfy the inner emptiness. He was also weighted down by all of his administrative duties. But what was disturbing his peace most was a nagging feeling that he should step out as an itinerant evangelist. This thought did not fit in with his plans at all. Itinerant evangelists travel from place to place preaching the gospel. DL was too attached to Chicago and the work he had built up to such immense proportions to leave it all behind.

About this time he noticed two ladies who always sat in the front row at church. They had the audacity to tell him they were praying for him to be baptized with the Holy Spirit and with fire. He greatly resented this at first, but their words went deep, and soon a great hunger was born in his heart.

"I began to cry out as I never did before. I really felt that I did not want to live if I could not have this power for service."[2] But in spite of great agonizing growing ever more intense, nothing happened. There was a block in the way. For love of the mighty work going on in his beloved Farwell Hall, Moody was resisting the inner call of God to go out and preach the gospel over the whole land.

There's no saying how long the struggle would have gone on if a great and tragic event hadn't overtaken Moody and many others. On Sunday, October 8, 1871, at the end of the service, the rude clanging of a fire bell shattered the solemnity. Then other bells were tolling, obviously sending out a warning of some kind. The meeting closed without panic, but as the congregation went out, utter chaos and terror met them. Flames were leaping up to the sky like giant serpents; not one building was ablaze, but building after building, whole streets were engulfed. Huge daggers of sparks shot out, then floated through pluming smoke; sharp cracks punctured the insidious hissing of steam; gas mains exploded and started new fires; the streets became hot under the running feet of panic-stricken citizens. Nineteenth-century fire fighting equipment was hopelessly inadequate to quell the littlest of the blazes; but still the bells rang, as though noise could do what the pathetic little spurts and dribbles of water couldn't.

The great fire of Chicago was to last until Wednesday. Once again, Farwell Hall, along with much of Chicago, was burned to cinders. Not only that, Moody lost his home, and had to endure the agony of not knowing for a time whether his family had perished or not.

Emotionally shocked, Moody went to New York to try and raise funds for rebuilding, but had little success. And still he was resisting the conviction of the Spirit concerning God's call to itinerant evangelism, and still he was in a spiritual desert. But then at last, on one of New York's busy streets, he gave in—and knew that God had met him! Said Moody, rushing back to his room, alone before the Lord, "I had such an experience of His love that I had to ask Him to stay His hand."

He picked up the pieces of the Chicago work, but deliberately held back from the administration, and kept ready for whatever "marching orders" God might send him.

In the summer he decided to go to Britain on his own to "rest and study the English Christians." His intention was not to preach, but he soon found he was getting invitations. While in Dublin, a friend said to him, almost casually, "Moody, the world has yet to see what God will do with a man fully consecrated to Him."

The remark registered, and over the next weeks Moody

resolved, "By the Holy Spirit in me, I will be that man!"

A little later he was asked to preach at a London Congregational church. The morning meeting seemed dead. However, unknown to Moody, there was a housebound invalid member of the church who had been praying for years for Moody to come, and hearing at Sunday lunch that the very object of her prayers was now in her chapel, praised the Lord and set herself to pray some more. That night, what a difference! All through the message there was an atmosphere that spoke of the Spirit's presence. At the end of the message, Moody made the invitation that those who wanted to receive Christ should stand. So many stood (it seemed like everyone present) he was convinced they had not understood. He explained more fully what repentance and faith meant, and then asked those who still wanted to receive Christ to come to the "inquiry room" adjoining. To his amazement, the huge crowd all followed him. Still wanting to make sure of things, he again stressed what coming to Christ involved and suggested they should return the next night to have a further talk with their own minister.

On the following Tuesday, he had an urgent wire to come back to the chapel because more people had come on Monday than had come on Sunday. He ended up conducting a week's meetings which resulted in 400 additions to the membership of that church.

Though not widely known, Moody was gathering something of a reputation in Britain, and he sailed back to the states under the firm impression that he had received three definite invitations and promises of support for a British campaign. In fact, he was taking too much for granted. Nevertheless, once back in Chicago he began to plan a British evangelistic tour from his end, blissfully trusting that all was being planned on his behalf at the British end. He wrote no letters to clarify what was happening, nor received any. He did have a couple of imploring requests from a British YMCA secretary, a young chemist, but did not take a great deal of notice feeling that the kind of resources and contacts needed for what was in mind would be beyond the inexperienced, unknown, Englishman. As with Moorhouse, Moody was misjudging which Englishman God would choose to bless him by!

So it was that on June 17, 1873, Moody arrived at Liverpool, England, with Sankey and their two families, to be greeted by his old friend Moorhouse with the news that, of the three expected supporters of his first full-scale British mission, two were dead and the third obviously didn't know anything about it. The shock of the traveling evangelists was probably only marginally less than that of a young chemist from the York YMCA when he was handed a telegram tersely asking: *Moody here are you ready for him?* Moody had decided after all that maybe *that* was the door the Lord was opening into England—"though it's only ajar," he admitted.

Three days later the young man, George Bennett, found what he had let himself in for as he breathlessly tried to keep up with Moody's breakneck pace. Halls booked, posters printed, clergy alerted—it was one huge rush. Things got under way on the Sunday morning at a Congregational chapel, given without enthusiasm by the deacons because their own minister was away. The service was not a great success. The afternoon was in the Corn Exchange, and on the neutral territory things were easier, the atmosphere more relaxed. The following week's meetings seemed to produce little impact. But then on the second Wednesday, the dam burst, and the pent-up blessing that had quietly been building began to flow. The Wesleyan chapel superintendent found himself weeping with joy. They moved on to the Baptist chapel, and there the minister, a scholarly, godly man, entered into a new dimension of ministry when he learned "about conversion . . . the gathering of sinners about Christ." He was F.B Meyer, whose books, still in print, continue to bless thousands.

The evangelists moved northeast to Sunderland, where they were not greatly successful, and to Newcastle where they were. One thing came out of the Sunderland meetings that stuck, though, and that was the slogan coined by the local minister to disarm criticism of Sankey's participation. "Mr. Moody will preach and Mr. Sankey will *sing* the Gospel."

Sankey's songs charmed everyone, and public demand was such that, though one publisher turned the idea down and lost a fortune, a 16-page pamphlet of "Sacred Songs and Solos" was soon on every drawing room piano. In the next 50 years the various editions are reckoned to have sold between 50 and 80 *million* copies; Moody and Sankey never received a cent of the royalties personally, ploughing all the profits into Christian work.

While still in Newcastle, Moody received an invitation to preach in Edinburgh, Scotland. He was not at all happy about it. From all he knew of the dour religion north of the border he felt he had a good chance of being eaten along with the Scots' porridge. But always a man for a challenge, and even more a man to sense the leading of God's Spirit, he accepted.

From the opening day of the Edinburgh campaign, November 23, 1873, it seemed as though the whole of Scotland wanted to hear the evangelists. They went from strength to strength, and not only in Edinburgh. Glasgow, Scotland's other great city, received them with open arms, as did many smaller places. People came from all over the ancient kingdom. Against the dark background of Knox's austere Calvinism, Moody's preaching sparkled and shone like a brilliant colored light. The dry bones of Scottish religion fairly rattled together, clothed with the warm human flesh of the American's anecdotal style, and filled with life by the Holy Spirit, and all to the accompaniment of Sankey's "kist o' whistles," as the Scots dubbed his reed organ. The triumph of the singing was remarkable, given that for many in the Scottish church "human" songs were banned. Even one of their most gifted hymn writers, Horatius Bonar, (who with his younger brother Andrew became a warm supporter of the evangelists) was not allowed to used his own hymns in his own church. But Sankey won them all over, especially when he composed on the spot a tune for a poem he had found in a magazine, singing in a way that had even Moody near to tears—"There were ninety and nine . . . " That song became as near a "hit" as any hymn could.

Throughout the summer of 1874 Scotland was alive to the sound of Sankey's music and Moody's preaching. But there had to be progress. After missions in Ireland, Manchester, Sheffield, and Birmingham, it was London. The question for everyone was: Could what had happened in the North happen in the capital? There were great preachers here already, notably Moody's early model, C.H. Spurgeon, who drew 5,000 hearers to every service. Would anyone take any notice of the strange Yankees?

The mission began in the huge Agricultural Hall adapted to seat 15,000 people. Soon the seating was found inadequate and was increased to 20,000.

Moody warned there would be criticism, and so it proved. Some newspapers were fair, others were not. Some churchmen were offended, but many supported. Gladstone, until recently Prime Minister, supported Moody and even sat on the platform.

Then Moody moved from the middle-class district of the Agricultural Hall to reach the lower and upper classes. (England was very class-conscious in the nineteenth century.) The next phase of his mission produced an extraordinary feat. He would preach in the East End in the early part of the evening and then after a cross-city dash in a carriage, at the Opera House in the West End in the latter half. The contrast in audiences must have been great. At one hour he would be preaching to farmers and the next to duchesses. Yet the miracle is, he reached the hearts of both.

One evening Sankey was very nervous when he found out that the Princess of Wales had come. Moody took it in his stride, stuffed his pockets with his notes as casually as ever, and preached in his usual way. Queen Victoria, however, declined to attend, despite a charming invitation from one of her ladies of the bedchamber.

One very out-of-the-ordinary request came to the evangelist to speak at England's most famous school, Eton, where the cream of Britain's leaders have received their education for centuries past. The invitation unleashed a huge controversy that even led to questions being raised in Britain's Upper House of Parliament, the Lords, much to the scorn of the press. But the most significant thing about it was not to be known at the time. And that was that one of the schoolboy attenders was C.T. Studd, son of a recent convert. And Charlie Studd would be making his own huge impact on the Christian world within a few years.

At last, in July 1875, the time came for the mission to end. Moody had captured all of Britain's heart. There had been nothing like it since Wesley's day. Chairing the farewell meeting, the determined old campaigner Lord Shaftesbury paid tribute. Good-byes brought tears to many eyes. But Moody was yearning for Chicago. It had been a gruelling two-year period and he wanted home. He returned, 38 years old, matured, unspoiled, the fiery evangelist who had learned his craft and practiced it with integrity, and received the blessing which he would be the first to say was to God's glory alone.

Moody and Sankey stepped off the ocean liner *Spain* in New York harbor to find they were famous men. In the eyes of their countrymen they had returned victorious or notorious, depending on the point of view, but either way men to be interviewed, talked about, invited here, there, and everywhere. But Moody had one great priority: he must go home to Northfield.

There he found his welcome warm and happy. But one

thing bothered him. His family and friends were still Unitarian and determined to stay so. After the heady excitement of London and preaching to royalty he made his next campaign right there, almost in his own backyard. His joy knew no bounds when his beloved mother and brother Samuel confessed Christ. The prophet had received honor in his own country and praised God for a family secure in Christ.

Now he was free to tackle America, and over the next seven years he poured himself into campaign after campaign in one state after the other. The British success proved to be no passing phenomenon attributable to the novelty of Yanks abroad. Whether it was New York, Chicago (where his campaign ran alongside the World's Fair), or Philadelphia, the people kept coming. There were special halls built to house the crowds, remarkable conversions and ardent supporters spanning the social range from the pickpocket who returned the watch he had stolen at the meeting, to Hiram Camp, who had probably made the watch, for he was founder of the biggest timepiece company in America.

Everywhere, Moody powered on at the same rocketing speed. He drove a horse and buggy so fast to a meeting that his passenger, soloist Philip Bliss, had to lie down to recover before he could sing.

But the huge campaigns with their thousands of converts were not the only things that occupied him. Conscious of his own lack of education, which he considered had been a handicap all his life, he began two Christian schools in his home town of Northfield, one for girls and the other for boys. He spent as much time there as he could, making them as much like family homes as was possible. The money came partly from his appeal to all sorts for funds (he was never afraid to ask a rich businessman for money, believing he was doing a service in directing money where it would do good) and partly from the profits from the sales of the songbook. He would point at the schools and say, "Sankey sang them up!"

What about Chicago? The tug on his heart strings from his old home country was too much for him, and as much as he loved Chicago and supported absolutely the work he had begun there, indeed beginning new work later with the famous Moody Bible Institute, his roots were deep in the subsoil of Northfield. He was still a farmer's boy at heart, and when he traveled, his letters home were full of inquiries about heifers and wheat and chickens. The ties with home were all the stronger now that he had a family growing fast.

Not that Northfield was simply a place to retire to for rest. There were the schools, of course, but in addition he also began a Christian convention. It was destined to play a big part in the future missionary expansion as the clear call to take the gospel to the uttermost parts of the earth was sounded out there against a background of intense prayer.

Soon it became clear that insistent calls to return to Britain could not be denied any longer. And so in 1881 he found himself stepping off the gangplank at Liverpool again. He had not been forgotten. Even the Customs officers came to shake him warmly by the hand.

With a few breaks in between, this visit was to last three years. The return was no let-down. Scotland was not as warmly responsive, it is true, mainly because disunity had tarnished the church's life since last time, but there were phenomenal happenings elsewhere.

Perhaps most significant of all in its long-term effects was the evangelists' visit to Cambridge at the invitation of the students. Conscious of his lack of learning, Moody was not at all willing to go, but go he did. In spite of the tormenting the students gave the pair at their first meeting (Sankey was almost in tears) soon the budding academics were listening intently. One of the ringleaders of the teasing saw Moody privately and then was converted. Seven young men, including the Studd brothers, sons of the race-going convert from Moody's former mission, became known as the "Cambridge Seven," who surrendered all to Christ in order to go out on the mission field. Their action made an enormous impression, and the repercussions still vibrate today. C.T. Studd, a cricket international, became the founder of the Worldwide Evangelization Crusade through which tens of thousands all over the world have come to know Christ.

Missions overseas, in fact, became a major emphasis in Moody's life. He himself almost went to India, but was prevented by doctors who advised his health would not stand the strain. Students also became an increasing part of his audience, and this man, who, to the day of his death, could not write a letter without ink-potfuls of spelling mistakes, won the minds as well as the hearts of the brilliant young intellectuals with his simple telling of the gospel.

As the years went on, Moody became increasingly concerned to see the church living in unity. He hated division, and though he never compromised truth, he had a broad enough grasp of it to see that individual interpretations should not be a bar to fellowship. He won the hearts of leaders of all denominations because they never felt threatened by him. He genuinely loved them and wanted to see all churches built up.

The years rolled on. There were grandchildren whom he loved and who loved him, still the great practical joker; there was sadness too, with deaths in his own family circle. But he himself seemed he would go on forever, preaching with as much power and with a scarcely less punishing schedule than 20 or 30 years before. But he was a big man, almost certainly by modern standards, overweight. His heart was wearing under the strain.

In fact he had been warned by a doctor in England that he must ease up. However, when the ship returning to America almost sunk, DL decided that heart pains or no heart pains, the gospel was too urgent to be given short measure. It must be an all-out effort to the end.

It was almost inevitable then that something in his mighty

frame would have to crack at some time. In a campaign in Kansas he became so unwell he had to withdraw, and he took the long journey back to Northfield quite ill. When the news was out, letters poured in, assuring him of prayer, and there were many, many heaven-directed petitions passionately pleaded from thousands of Christian lips for this giant of evangelism. But the Lord had decided it was time to take his servant home, and on December 22, 1899, the most effective gospel voice of two English-speaking nations was still.

Moody had made his own summing-up of the event years before: "Some day you will read in the papers that D.L. Moody of East Northfield is dead. Don't you believe a word of it! At that moment I shall be more alive than I am now. I shall have gone up higher—that is all; gone out of this old clay tenement into a house that is immortal, a body that death cannot touch, and sin cannot taint, a body like unto his own glorious body. I was born of the flesh in 1837. I was born of the Spirit in 1856. That which is born of the flesh may die; that which is born of the Spirit will live for ever."[7]

For further reading: *Moody Without Sankey* by J.C. Pollock (Hodder & Stoughton)
Moody: the Biography by J.C. Pollock (Moody Press)

Notes
1. J.C. Pollock, *Moody Without Sankey* (London: Hodder and Stoughton, 1963), p. 20.
2. W.R. Moody, *Life of D.L. Moody* (London: Morgan and Scott, 1900), p. 19.
3. Pollock, *Moody Without Sankey*, p. 29.
4. Moody, *Life of D. L. Moody*, p. 36.
5. Moody, *Life of D. L. Moody*, p. 36.
6. Pollock, *Moody Without Sankey*, p.57.
7. Moody, *Life of D. L. Moody*, p. 7.

William Tyndale

A little less than one hour ago I touched the most valuable small object I have ever touched in my life. With a nominal insurance value of more than a quarter of a million dollars, no real price can in fact be put upon it, for it is one of the world's unique and irreplaceable treasures. But even if it were to be valued at a million, two million, or more, its cost would still defy all figures. For it has cost blood.

What we are talking about is a book, a Bible—a New Testament, to be more exact. Measuring only the length and breadth of a good-sized pocket diary, but many times thicker, its clear, clean, black type is as sharp and bright as the day it was printed in the German city of Worms in 1526. It is the work of William Tyndale, who saw it as his life's calling from God to give the ordinary Englishman what he had never had before: the Scriptures in his mother tongue. His dedication to the task cost him his comfort in this life and a premature entry into the next.

The historic Worms Testament resides in the vault of the Baptist College, Bristol, England, and it is a mere dozen miles from there that William Tyndale's vision was born while he was a young schoolmaster privately tutoring in the country house called Little Sodbury (which still stands today). His life before then had been fairly uneventful for a clever young man of his time. Son of a comfortably off yeoman-farmer family from Gloucestershire, he had studied at Oxford and Cambridge and been ordained into the priesthood. Not that his official studies were particularly inspiring. He said himself, "In the Universities they have ordained that no man shall look on the scripture, until he be noselled in heathen learning eight or nine years, and armed with false principles, with which he is clean shut out of the understanding of the scripture."

But the lectures and official courses were one thing, what the students got up to on their own quite another. And in the English universities of the early 1500s plenty was going on. Erasmus, who made the first printed edition of the Greek New Testament, had lectured there; John Colet had unfolded the pure truths of Paul's epistles; students were becoming excitedly aware that in Germany a bold monk, Martin Luther, had thumbed his nose at the Pope—and was still barely surviving. There were young men studying who were already moving on the reforming swell that was disturbing the lifeless calm of the medieval church, men such as Thomas Bilney, Robert Barnes, and John Frith. As William began to read the Scriptures for himself, his love for them began to grow, and his conviction that here was the final authority for faith. So although we don't know of any dramatic moment of conversion, we can take it that by the time William took up his job at

Little Sodbury, 1522, he was already spiritually alive and ready for what the Lord had in store for him as a lifework.

The year before he left Cambridge, however, he witnessed something that gave ominous warning of things to come. There, in the center of the university town supposedly devoted to advancement in learning, a great bonfire was lit. Luther's works, as many as could be found, provided the fuel.

Little Sodbury Manor is a color calendar photographer's dream—everything that goes to make up the romantic person's notion of Olde Worlde England. The yellow ochre of Cotswold stone, mellowed by moist breezes, colored by lichens, decorated by ivy, makes the long two-story building fairly glow with charm. Four and a half centuries ago, the color would be sharper because the weathering would be less, and keeping warm in such a place, even with the huge open fires, would be something of a problem, but nevertheless it must have been a pleasant place to be.

The owner, Tyndale's employer, was Sir John Walsh, a man of about 35, who had been at the court of the current British monarch, Henry VIII. He had several children, the oldest only seven. Tyndale's massive intellect was not likely to be overstretched.

William found other things to do. He must have kept up his own studying for a start. Also, he sometimes preached. But it was the chatter at meals that shaped his future.

Sir John, as a man of substance, frequently had important people, including high-up churchmen, around his table, and the conversation often turned to Erasmus, Luther, and the encroachment of "heresy" in the church. William would pitch in with his say, and prove his points from Scripture with the sort of tactless "told-you-so" of youth that would tempt a saint to resentment. And these abbots and archdeacons were not that holy.

Although Sir John and his good lady rallied to William's defense, the eventual outcome was that William found himself having to answer to a charge of heresy at a meeting of clergy. Heresy was a particularly serious crime at this point in history when the established Catholic Church had enormous power. People who were accused of heresy were believed to hold to ideas that contradicted church teaching. If found guilty the accused might be barred from church membership, imprisoned, or even executed. William got off with a caution, but things were looking ominous. Unless he kept as quiet as a gatepost (which wasn't his nature) there was little doubt he would be in further trouble.

But the hostility of the clergy was bringing about the conception and gestation of an idea that was determined to be born. If ignorance of the Scriptures was the problem, with not just the people but even the priests sometimes unable to recite the Lord's Prayer, why not provide the English people with the Scriptures to read for themselves in their own tongue? The idea grew within William and would not go away. It all fell into place for him one day during a heated discussion with a learned churchman whose temperature was escalating into the thermometer-bursting danger zone as William pursued his relentless Scripture arguments in opposition to church decrees.

"We were better without God's law than without the pope's!" the overheated cleric snapped.

With scarcely less passion, and with a committed determination, Tyndale replied, "I defy the pope and all his laws. If God spare my life, ere many years I will cause a boy that driveth the plough shall know more of the scripture than thou dost."

With this resolution formed, William faced the practicalities. Where and how should he do the work? Little Sodbury was a pleasant enough place, and there was quiet for study, but he needed books. Beautiful Gloucestershire was too much in the backwoods. Anyway, he guessed his safety there was precarious at best. He decided to head for London. There was a new bishop there with something of a reputation for learning. If he could get a job as his chaplain, or something similar . . . .

He was disappointed. Bishop Cuthbert Tonstall was indeed a scholar, but sympathetic to a New Testament translation he was not, nor did he want to take on any more staff, thank you very much. But Tyndale should be able to find some sort of work in London, Tonstall assured him.

Next port of call was a friendly merchant, Humphrey Monmouth, who was showing signs of wanting church reform. He had heard Tyndale preach while the latter was waiting for his interview with the bishop, and was impressed. For six months, this layman did what the bishop wouldn't—gave bed and board to the would-be translator. Tyndale refused to take undue advantage of the generosity, however. Monmouth said later, "He studied most part of the day and of the night at his book, and he would eat but sodden meat by his good will, nor drink but small single beer."

Tyndale's thoughts about how best to fulfill his great project began to develop further. He saw in London the decadent pomp and worldly scheming of the priests and prelates. Given the spiritual and political state of England, what chance was there of ever getting his work printed, and even if printed, distributed? Precious little. But Germany . . . Luther was in Germany, and he had made a German New Testament. Things were dangerous there too, but at least there was the *possibility* that it could be done. And the printers of Germany; they were the inventors of the art. So, having, as he said, "understood at the last, not only that there was no room in my Lord of London's palace to translate the New Testament, but also that there was no place to do it in all England," Tyndale gathered up his Bibles and his work to date, went down to the wharf beside the Thames, and took ship for the Continent, arriving at Wittenberg, home of the Reformation, sometime in 1524.

To our loss, we know nothing of his stay there. We catch up with him a year or so later in Cologne, where he and another English reformer, William Roye, decided to make their base for getting the work completed. The actual translating work had been done. What they needed now was a printing press. Printer Peter Quentel obliged, and all looked to be going well until one of Luther's staunchest opponents, whose chief delight in life was to frustrate those he called heretics, chanced across them. He found out what was going on by getting the printers (and probably Roye) drunk with the local brew. He discovered to his horror there was a print-run of 3,000 half-way through the making. He quickly got an order from the magistrates halting the work, but Tyndale and Roye, getting wind of it, gathered up all the sheets printed so far and fled. Unfortunately, the zealous anti-Lutheran also took it on himself to write to Henry VIII in England to tell of his discovery, which meant that the alarm was raised in Tyndale's homeland that would make eventual distribution doubly dangerous and difficult.

Tyndale and Roye took refuge in Worms, the very same place where a few years before Luther had made his courageous stand for the gospel, his conscience captive to the Word of God. It seems appropriate that the first printed English version of the Word of God should see the light of day there, though it is unlikely that the thought crossed Tyndale's mind. He was more concerned about getting that same word into England. It is from this first printing that the Bristol Baptist College copy survives, "the greatest treasure of all English printed Bibles." Its survival is probably due to the fact that it did not immediately get shipped to England with the rest of the batch, for as we shall see, there were perils in store.

The first copies reached England around March 1526. How they came we're not quite sure. The easiest way was down the Rhine River to Cologne, but that would run head-long into the opposition of the man who closed down the printing there. Perhaps they went out through the trade fairs at Frankfort. One thing is fairly certain—when they came across the English channel, they would be well disguised, hidden in all the ingenious ways perfected by smugglers through the centuries.

The book was circulated quietly and cautiously among those eager for reform. By midsummer, the bishops knew it had arrived. They held an official meeting to decide what to do. Then on October 25 Bishop Tonstall called all the London booksellers together and warned them against importing "Lutheran" books. He also issued an injunction to his arch-deacons in trenchant terms: "Certain children of iniquity, maintainers of Luther's sect, blinded by extreme wickedness, declining from the way of truth and the orthodox faith, have with crafty trickery translated the holy gospel of God into our vulgar English tongue . . . many books, containing the pestilent and pernicious poison in the vulgar tongue have been dispersed."

The archdeacons were commanded to call in within 30 days all copies under pain of excommunication and suspicion of heresy. The Archbishop of Canterbury, Warham, issued similar orders, and so there took place at Saint Paul's Cross in London, a massive public burning. An unknown quantity of Tyndale's first edition went up in flames. Monmouth, Wiliam's London benefactor, was there, and heard Tonstall preach that Tyndale had "naughtily translated" the New Testament into English.

However, forbidden fruit always tastes sweeter, and the burning, if anything, increased the demand. In fact, by mid-November a pirate edition printed in Antwerp was on the London streets. Cardinal Wolsey, King Henry's chief henchman and the most powerful man in England next to the king, traced through his ambassador the Antwerp printer responsible, and eventually prevailed upon the local authorities to seize the copies and burn them there. To his dismay, however, another Dutch printer took over, and still the books came. Archbishop Warham decided to buy up as many as he could (getting the other bishops to subscribe to the tune of nearly 100 dollars) which as he later realized actually encouraged the printing by putting money into the pockets of the printers.

While these first editions of the English New Testament were being burned, it was frustrating, but no more than that. But soon, inevitably, it was the readers who came under attack. In November 1527, Bilney (who had been at Cambridge with Tyndale) was arrested, and though he renounced Tyndale, was made to carry a bundle of sticks to a book burning and throw it on the fire as a sign of his humiliation. Then early the next year a vigorous search for the English New Testament in Oxford led to a number, including John Frith, being thrown into prison in appalling conditions for several months. Three of them perished there. In February, Bishop Tonstall commenced a great drive against heretics, so that by March 1528 his prisons were full.

Meanwhile, back on the Continent, Tyndale was busy. His New Testament complete, he was writing tracts and treatises of various kinds, all of them pushing forward the contentions of the reformation and criticizing the un-scriptural doctrines of Rome. As these began to circulate in Britain, so the fury of the church hierarchy increased.

By now, Tyndale was in Antwerp, and separated from Roye who turned out to be an unsatisfactory helper. Wolsey's ambassador in Antwerp, a man named Hackett, was given the job of trying to track Tyndale down, but the reformer proved too elusive for him at this time. Whatever Tyndale had to do to avoid detection, he did not let it interfere with his work. His occupation now was with the Old Testament.

This was quite an achievement, for he had to start right from scratch and learn Hebrew first, never having studied it before. His access to translation aids and dictionaries must have been very limited. It is possible that in Antwerp he may have had some help from Jewish rabbis. But his chief aid was his own prodigous God-given talent for languages. He completed the Pentateuch (the first five books of the Old Testament) and then took the manuscripts by ship to Hamburg, probably to shake Hackett off his tail. Then tragedy: Tyndale was shipwrecked. His own life was saved, but he lost his precious manuscripts, as well as his reference books. It meant he had to start all over again. In Hamburg, the slow, laborious work was made easier by the help of Miles Coverdale, who was later to produce his own translation of the Bible which would incorporate Tyndale's work. Once the translation was complete, William bravely returned to Antwerp to get the work printed, and it was not long before this too was circulating in England, much to the dismay of the English rulers, both of church and state. It could only be a matter of time before someone was actually put to death for their allegiance to the reformed cause.

And so it proved. In March 1530, within two months of the publication of Genesis, a friend of Tyndale, Thomas Hitton, went to the stake at Maidstone, condemned by Archbishop Warham and Bishop Fisher.

The controversy was now full-blown. Henry VIII called to the palace at Westminster an assembly of church leaders to discuss the problem of "Lutheran" books. The outcome was a prohibition against the free circulation of Old or New Testaments, and a condemnation of a long list of works from Tyndale and other writers. Henry described Tyndale's writings as "blasphemous and pestiferous English books."

At this stage another man took over the high office of Wolsey (who had fallen from favor). This man was to become the chief enemy of Tyndale. They were to wage a ceaseless war of words, and if he could have gotten hold of Tyndale he would surely have seen him to the stake himself. But the name of this immovable foe is a surprise. It is Thomas More, who has romantic hold on people's imaginations as "The Man for All Seasons," the cultured family man, the civilized scholar, whose integrity cost him his life. The romantic notion is not a lie; it is simply one-sided. His home was the scene of domestic bliss; it was also the place where more than one suspected heretic was "examined." He is officially canonized as Saint Thomas More, yet he fully supported the killing of people who believed differently. It is sad that such a great man could read Tyndale's books and translations for himself and see nothing good in them at all. Typical of More's reactions is his comment on Tyndale's exposition of Jonah: "Jonah was never so swallowed up with the whale, as by the delight of that book a man's soul may be so swallowed up by the devil."

One of the men examined in More's house was James Baynham, a lawyer. He confessed to owning five of Tyndale's books, but recanted and, after the usual humiliation of having to carry a bundle of sticks to Saint Paul's Cross for the book burning and a fine of 20 pounds, was set free. But then conscience overtook him, and one Sunday morning he entered church carrying for all to see Tyndale's New Testament and another of the reformer's works. With tears, he publicly withdrew his recantation. He was seized and convicted of being a relapsed heretic. On April 30, 1532, he was burned at the stake at Smithfield. He was the tenth martyr in two and a quarter years.

Another to pay the ultimate price was Tyndale's dearest friend, John Frith. Daring to return to England, he was captured and put in the Tower of London. There he stayed for five months, and then rather indiscreetly wrote at the request of a friend his views on the Lord's Supper, which unfortunately fell into the hands of Thomas More. This put him immediately into danger. Tyndale in Antwerp knew what was going on, and wrote a wise, loving letter to his friend. More, meanwhile, was trying to answer Frith. He tackled him on the literature he and

Tyndale produced. Frith's reply smacked of Luther's famous words: "Until we see some means found by which a reasonable reformation may be had, and sufficient instruction for the poor commoners, I assure you I neither will nor can cease to speak; for the word of God boileth in my blood like a fervent fire."

Eventually Frith was brought to trial and condemned. Many were sorry for him, and he even was deliberately given a chance to escape, which he refused, because, he said, he must testify to his faith and not betray the cause of God.

Just before his execution day, he received another letter from Tyndale encouraging him. "Dearly beloved, be of good courage . . . follow the example of all your other dear brethren which chose to suffer in hope of a better resurrection."

So it seemed the persecution would never stop. Tyndale did, however, have some sympathizers. Cromwell (not, of course, Oliver, who belongs to the next century) became strong once Henry had broken with the church of Rome over the matter of his divorce, the same event that caused More's eventual downfall. Cromwell was kindly disposed toward Tyndale, and worked hard to try to get him to return to England. He sent an agent of his, Stephen Vaughan, who actually met Tyndale and talked the matter over with him, and a number of letters were exchanged. But Tyndale did not trust the invitation—and probably rightly. Too many of his friends had perished, even though they had been promised safe conduct.

But in truth the storm was beginning to calm in England. The king's divorce had severed him from the church of Rome, and though it did not make a Protestant out of him, yet those with reformation at their heart were beginning to make their influence felt. But the change was gradual, and the times were still dangerous. To this gradual change was added an irony—that as things became a little easier in England, things were becoming more precarious in Antwerp.

The problem was that it was not wholly up to the city

fathers what went on in their town. The Netherlands was part of the Holy Roman Empire, and the Emperor had his own edicts out concerning heretics. Tyndale had been relatively safe by living in the English House, owned by the English merchants who, by reason of their commercial importance, were given immunity against various laws. The head of this community was Thomas Poyntz, a great supporter of Tyndale.

All was well until an Englishman, Henry Phillips, arrived on the scene. He seemed to come from nowhere, but somehow Tyndale, who one would have thought would be cautious in making friendships, took to him. In fact, Tyndale trusted Phillips enough to show him his books and manuscripts. The two men would often dine together. Poyntz was suspicious, but accepted Tyndale's reassurances.

Phillips seemed to have no shortage of money, and dropped hints to Poyntz about his ability to pay for things. It was only when it was too late Poyntz realized he was in fact being offered money to betray Tyndale.

If only Poyntz (and Tyndale) had known this was indeed a traitor in their midst. Phillips was from a landed family and had fled England in disgrace, having gambled away money entrusted to him by his father. His solution to his personal financial crisis was to become the apprehender of the Bible translating heretic. Who paid Phillips for pursuing Tyndale has never been discovered, but it was plainly someone who counted Tyndale a very great enemy, and hated him and what he stood for sufficiently to go to great lengths and expense to get rid of him.

Phillips took himself off to the court of Brussels, and brought back from there the procurer-general, the emperor's attorney, the essential man if Tyndale was to be charged and brought to trial. He then set about continuing to develop his relationship with Tyndale.

Once again they agreed to dine together, and at dinner time Phillips called. The entrance to the English House led into a narrow passage, one had to walk through single file. Tyndale indicated that Phillip should go first, but in a show of deference, Phillips insisted Tyndale take the lead. What the reformer did not know was that posted each side of the passage a little way along were two officers. As Phillips and Tyndale approached the spot, Phillips, who was the taller of the two, pointed down to Tyndale's head, which, like the kiss of Judas, gave the officers the indication they were going for the right man. They arrested him and hauled him off to the procurer-general's house. The officers then went round to Tyndale's lodging and took all his books and things. Tyndale was taken to the castle of Vilford, 18 miles away. The date was May 21, 1535. Tyndale was to spend the next 16 months in prison.

Poyntz was horrified to find what had happened. The good man pulled out all the stops to help his friend. Dissatisfied with the authorities in Antwerp, whom he felt should take action because the rights and privileges of the English House had been abused, he decided he would appeal to the King of England, Henry VIII. Admittedly, it did not seem a very hopeful move but the attempt must be made. After all, Tyndale was still a British subject, and though the king's opposition to the things Tyndale stood for was well-known, by a bizarre twist of events, the Catholic defender of the faith was now monarch of a protestant realm. Also, Cromwell was quite favorably disposed to the reformers though as an astute politician, he would not be an open supporter.

Poyntz fretted as he waited. Nothing seemed to happen, and he wrote passionately to his brother in England to do some badgering on his behalf. At last he was given letters to try to obtain his friend's release. He threw himself wholeheartedly into the task; the net result was that instead of Tyndale being freed, Poyntz was imprisoned. Once again, the evil move behind the arrest was Phillips.

There followed a harrowing three months in jail, and the

prospect of death loomed closer. Poyntz decided he would have to make a break for it, which he successfully accomplished. How he managed it is obscure, but slip away he did, and although a search party went after him, he knew the country well, made good his flight to the coast, and from there to England. The cost of his friendship with Tyndale was high enough already, but there was more. Banished from the Netherlands for life, he forfeited his business, his goods, and his home. Also, his Dutch wife refused for many years to join him, and the former wealthy merchant lived out the rest of his life in poverty. But he never expressed, it seems, any resentment.

All this time Tyndale was still enduring the uncertainty of his fate. In his prison, built in imitation of the French Bastille, conditions began to take their toll as the summer moved into winter. He wrote a touching plea to his captors. "I beg your Lordship, and that by the Lord Jesus, that if I am to remain here through the winter, you will request the commissary to send me, from the goods of mine which he has, a warmer cap; for I suffer greatly from cold in the head, and am afflicted by a perpetual catarrh, which is much increased in this cell; a warmer coat also, for this which I have is very thin; a piece of cloth too to patch my leggings. My overcoat is worn out; my shirts are also worn out . . . . And I ask to be allowed to have a lamp in the evening; it is indeed wearisome sitting alone in the dark. But most of all, I beg and beseech your clemency . . . to have the Hebrew Bible, Hebrew grammar, and Hebrew dictionary . . . . "[1] Sadly, it is unlikely the last request was granted, and so we are denied a completed Tyndale Old Testament.

Tyndale's trial took the form of a long, protracted debate with three of the top theologians from Louvain University, which was a center of anti-Lutheranism. Tyndale defended himself with skill, and as always was the master of Scripture, but the result was inevitable. They failed to get him to renounce his beliefs, and he failed to win them to his side (though along the way, his keeper, the keeper's daughter, and others were converted; Tyndale's prison witness was as sharp as the great apostle Paul's). The sorry verdict was given: Tyndale was guilty of heresy and was to be degraded from the priesthood and handed over to the secular power for execution.

The degradation ceremony, held in the town square, was a miserable affair. It was ordination in reverse. Bishops sat on a platform, and Tyndale was led to them clothed in his clerical garb. Kneeling in front of them, his hands were scraped with a knife symbolizing the taking away of the anointing oil. Next, bread and wine were placed in his hands and then officiously removed. Lastly, his vestments were stripped off him one by one. The black ceremony completed, Tyndale was handed over to the procurer-general; the church had finished with him, now the state must do its part.

It was two months before the sentence of execution was carried out—an unusually long delay. We can only guess what went through his mind in those wearisome weeks. One thing we can be sure of—never at any time did he think of abandoning his stand. Perhaps his most likely regret was those remaining untranslated books of the Old Testament. Some other mind than his would have to be applied to the task.

But at last, sometime in early October 1536, Tyndale's final day on earth dawned. As the sun climbed into the autumn sky, the early mist, ominously like a death shroud, slipped away. The great reformer was led out to an open space near the southern gate of Vilvorde where barricades arranged in a rough circle kept back spectators. In the circle, two great beams were set up in the shape of a cross and through holes in the cross beam, a chain and a rope were threaded. Brushwood and logs lay around the foot of the cross.

The procurer-general and his colleagues took their places in front, and Tyndale, having refused one last chance to recant, was led to the stake and bound to it by chains around his feet and the chain through the holes in the cross fastened his neck. The brushwood and logs, with straw and gun powder, were then heaped around him to make a kind of hut. From this tabernacle of death, Tyndale lifted up his face to heaven with one last, heartfelt prayer. "Lord, open the King of England's eyes!"

The procurer-general gave his signal, and the executioner quickly tightened the rope and held it until he was sure his victim was dead. Then handed a lighted torch, he set the straw and brushwood ablaze.

The courageous translator was dead. Many who espoused his cause were also dead. But their cause triumphed. Tyndale's last prayer was answered within the year, for in 1537 the very first English translation of the Bible printed with Royal permission was published. Called Matthew's Bible, it contained all of Tyndale's translation as far as he had completed it. And when the Authorized King James Bible was published in 1611, that too, was largely Tyndale's work. While new, accurate translations continue to be published to this day, the work of the man who wanted common people to be able to read Scripture in their own language remains the standard by which new works are judged.

For further reading: *William Tyndale,* by J.F. Mozley
(SPCK, London)

Notes
1. J.F. Mozley, *William Tyndale* (London: SPCK, 1937), p. 334.

4

John Wesley

The sleeping little boy was suddenly awakened out of his dreams by a crashing and banging; sitting up, startled, he heard other noises—screams, shouts of panic. The room felt very hot.

"Run, John, run!" someone was yelling more urgently than he'd ever heard his name called before.

Heart beating, he jumped out of bed and ran to the door, wrenching it open to be met by a blazing wall of fire. For the first time he realized ,fully what was wrong. The house was ablaze—and there was no way down the staircase, which was almost gone, hungry flames lapping where steps should be. He quickly shut the door to stop the onward march of the flames, and tried to work out what to do. He ran to a chest, and using all the strength he could muster from his tiny frame he struggled to push it under the high window. Then he clambered on top of the chest, and somehow or other got the window open. Below, two men saw his nightgowned shape and ran. Climbing one on top of the other, they lifted him to safety just before the thatched roof collapsed in a lurid, orange flood of flame. They delivered him safely to his father, the rector of the parish Church of Epworth, who had only just committed the soul of his infant son to God, scarcely believing that the little lad could survive such a dreadful fire.

The experience of John Wesley in February 1709 made an impression that was never to leave him. He described himself in later life as "a brand plucked out of the burning" (see Zech. 3:2), and was convinced it was all God's doing, that He must have a destiny for him to fulfill. And so it proved.

When the large Wesley family were able to meet as one unit again in the rebuilt rectory at the end of the year (until then they were dispersed around the village) Mrs. Susannah Wesley decided to take them in hand. Both she and her husband were very godly people, but she was one of those remarkable women who have the knack of controlling the reins despite whoever else is there.

"The first thing to be done with children is to conquer the will," she would say. So young John's rear end often smarted, but he learned to value disciplined living, and it was to be his characteristic ever after. Not that Susannah was all heavy hand; she had a cheerfulness and love that made John very fond of her. She also made religion real. When her husband was away and a not-very-good clergyman was substituting, she would hold services on Sunday evenings in her kitchen for the family and servants. But so popular were these meetings that the regulars all brought their friends, and there could be as many as 200 in attendance—which says something about the size of the kitchen.

John showed great promise as he grew up. It was the most natural thing to find himself going up to Oxford University when he was 17. That was in 1720. By 1725, still at Oxford, a new religious earnestness began to move him. He even had a go at converting a young man he saw at a funeral. Like so many brought up in Christian homes, he assumed that he himself already was a Christian. It was in that conviction he began to believe he was called to the ministry, and thus on September 19, 1725, he was ordained a deacon.

When his brother Charles joined him a year later, after a while they formed what they called "The Holy Club," then , with a few like-minded people, they set out to improve their lives in a way that would please God, filling their time with good works and acts of Christian devotion. The title was not their own, but given them by young men who found it odd that students would want to do anything more than enjoy themselves with the baser delights of a university city. Soon the guys had another name for these peculiar do-gooders: "Methodists." That came about from the simple fact that members of the club seemed so seriously methodical about everything they did. Apart from their rules for prayer and church going, they made regular visits to the prison and to the workhouse (where the poor were put by the authorities), and distributed clothes, food, prayerbooks, and Bibles to the poor.

John Wesley, always a believer in practicing what he preached, as leader of the group gave away all that he did not require for his immediate needs of food and clothing and books. In addition, the club members took it as their mission to convert the idle layabouts who formed a large slice of the student population—that was a part of their activities that didn't have spectacular success. But then how could it, when their leader, John, was having increasing problems about his own position before God? The truth was, with all his commendable diligence and zeal, he had no real assurance of salvation. The fact that he, as the other members of the club, spent an hour each morning and evening in prayer, recited a brief formal prayer three times a day, and monitored minutely his spiritual state, did nothing to give him joy or any sense of the love of God. As yet, he wasn't aware that real Christian experience *could* be different.

The club gradually broke up as the various members graduated and moved away. In 1735 John and Charles themselves left, not just Oxford, but England. America then was still under British rule, and Colonel James Oglethorpe, governor of Georgia, in London with several splendid Indians in tow, was wanting a new chaplain and staff to go out with him. The invitation appealed immensely to the Wesleys, so the Reverend John and the Reverend Charles Wesley found themselves in very short time on board the *Simmonds,* with a third Holy Club member, Benjamin Ingham. The poverty of John's spiritual understanding comes out in his explanation of his going: "My chief motive . . . is the hope of saving my own soul . . . I hope to learn the true sense of the gospel of Christ by preaching it to the heathen."

Almost as soon as they were cast off and floating gently down the Thames, John wasted no time on the ship in going around talking to people about their souls. As for his own spiritual discipline, he went into his strictest program yet. Renouncing meat and wine, he determined to live on rice and vegetables and biscuits. He did without supper altogether and made a deliberate decision not to enjoy even the sparse fare he did eat. Every hour of the day was to be filled with some task—from four in the morning till bedtime. Yet all was far from well inside his soul, and he wrote, "In vain have I fled from myself to America. I still groan under the intolerable weight of inherent misery . . . . Go where I will, I carry my hell about with me."

Crossing the Atlantic from east to west in winter in a sailing ship is a hazardous business. In those days, before radio and radar and stabilizers, it was guaranteed to give you the adventure of your life. Three furious gales hit them, one after the other, threatening to send the new missionary to the Indians to a wetter mission field among the fishes.

Controlling his erratic pen as best he could, he scratched in his diary "Storm greater: afraid!" At seven o'clock he went to a little group of travelers, a religious community called the Moravians from Germany, who were holding a meeting. At this time the force of the storm was beating up the sea to towering heights. Ben Ingham recalled, "The sea sparkled and smoked, as if it had been on fire. The air darted forth lightning; and the wind blew so fierce, that you could scarcely look it in the face and draw your breath." While the Moravians were singing a psalm, all of a sudden there was a mighty crack as the mainsail split as though blasted by an invisible giant's karate chop, and a Niagara of water cascaded between the decks. Panic was instantaneous among the passengers; broken planks and debris seemed to be awash everywhere. The Moravians looked up briefly and carried on singing.

Wesley was astounded. After the storm subsided, he asked one of them, "Were you not afraid?"

"I thank God, no," was the smiling reply.

"But were not your women and children afraid?"

"No, our women and children are not afraid to die."

It was a Christian approach to life Wesley had not encountered before. The sheer calmness was a sharp contrast to his frantic busyness and anxious activity. But more was to come from this strange sect to challenge the young missionary.

Once landed, he met a Moravian minister, Gottlieb Spangengburg, who, at 32, was one year younger than Wesley himself. Out of the blue, the man asked Wesley, "Do you know yourself? Have you the witness in yourself? Does the Spirit of God bear witness with your spirit that you are a child of God?"

Wesley was knocked off balance. He had no idea how to

reply. Spangengburg questioned further. "Do you know Jesus Christ?"

Still groping, the best Wesley could offer was, "I know He is the Saviour of the world."

Spangengburg pressed home his point.

"True, but do you know he has saved *you?*"

Completely thrown, Wesley stammered out, "I hope he has died to save me."

Spangengburg came back to his original question. "Do you know yourself?"

This time Wesley gave the answer Spangengburg desired to hear, and he desired to give. "I do." But he confessed in his *Journal* they were "vain words."

There is an old story of a minister who had scribbled in the margin of his sermon notes, "Argument weak—shout." Perhaps John Wesley was a man of too much integrity to consciously adopt such an approach, but it is quite likely that these spiritual uncertainties, which seemed to be increasing by the day, were part of the explanation for the almost fanatical zeal he poured into his new post. The trouble was that he seemed to upset almost everyone in so doing. He never succeeded in reaching the hearts of the Indians, who were quite unlike the "noble savages" he had met in the London home of General Oglethorpe, and he was so extreme in his church discipline, excluding people from communion and so on, that soon his congregation was sick of him and he was sick of them. His congregation dwindled, all kinds of complaints were laid concerning him, and he even had one irate woman attack him by biting his sleeve. It became abundantly clear that the whole mission would have to be given up as an abysmal failure.

On February 1, 1738, Wesley docked at Deal, Kent, defeated and dejected. On the journey back he had written, "I went to America to convert the Indians; but Oh! who shall convert me? Who, what, is he that will deliver me from this evil heart of unbelief?" Once landed, he repeated the same ago-nizing question in that day's *Journal:* "It is now two years and almost four months since I left my native country, in order to teach the Georgian Indians the nature of Christianity. But what have I learned myself in the meantime? Why, what I the least of all expected, that I, who went to America to convert others, was never myself converted to God."

But help was on the way! God's timetable, as always, was working out to the minute. It so happened that in making contact with a Moravian group meeting in the house of a Dutch family, he was introduced to a 26-year-old Moravian missionary, Peter Böhler, on his way out to Georgia, and he proved to be one of the wisest doctors of souls who ever was. He was certainly the man to help the tortured John Wesley, at any rate.

Having met him six days after docking, Wesley traveled to Oxford with Böhler on the 17 and spent the weekend in his company together with Charles. They had long conversations. The most puzzling thing for Wesley was Böhler's advice, "My brother, my brother, that philosophy of yours must be purged away!" Peter Böhler had discerned that mighty and marvelous though Wesley's learning was, it was a barrier to the simple faith that brings assurance of God's love. Wesley now under-stood that it was faith, justifying faith, that was his great lack. Oh, to *really believe* that Christ's death on the cross brought salvation as a gift to be received like a child would take a present from his father! But such simple trust eluded the Oxford scholar for a while yet.

His next meeting with Böhler was on March 5, and Wesley presented him with a problem. He was, he told his young teacher, fully persuaded about the need for faith, but he didn't have it yet. Shouldn't he give up preaching? Böhler strongly advised the opposite.

"Preach faith *till* you have it, and then, *because* you have it you *will* preach faith." It is advice some would query. But it proved to be absolutely right for Wesley. In fact, things began to happen that are inexplicable outside a recognition that God is sovereign and can do as He wills. People became converted under the unconverted Wesley!

At the end of the same month Wesley went to the Castle at Oxford and preached, then prayed, with a prisoner. The man became a Christian on the spot, trusting Christ for forgiveness.

But still Wesley himself was not able to have complete faith. He presented Böhler with another obstacle. Wasn't it a mistake to speak of an *instantaneous work* of conversion? Böhler replied that Wesley must search the Scriptures. Wesley "searched the Scriptures again touching this very thing, particularly the Acts of the Apostles: but to my utter astonishment, found scarce any instances there of any other than *instantaneous* conversion."

But Wesley's objections were still not finished. What about today? Surely things didn't happen that way now? Peter Böhler smiled. He could produce living witnesses, and Wesley should hear for himself. As good as his word, a little while later he produced four English Moravians who each gave their testimony to John and Charles. John was moved to tears, and in a private conversation with Böhler said he would ask no more questions except how should he attain to such a faith. He had not sinned as much as others. Böhler told him that not to believe in the Saviour was sinning enough.

It seems hard that poor Wesley had to go through such agonies at what was truly within a child's grasp. But no doubt it all helped to make him that much more effective an evangelist later. But at the time it must have seemed to him that the peace that comes from truly knowing Christ is Saviour was going to elude him forever, especially as the time for Böhler's departure was near. From the port of Southampton the German sent one last word of encouragement: "Delay not, I beseech you, to believe in *your* Jesus Christ."

A few days later, Wednesday May 24, Wesley found the sunshine of God's love at last.

In the morning he read from his Bible, "You are not far from the kingdom of God" (see Mark 12:34) and in the afternoon he heard an anthem in Saint Paul's Cathedral based on Psalm 130 that seemed to speak to his need exactly. But these things were but God's preparation for what was to follow.

"In the evening I went very unwillingly to a society in Aldersgate Street, where one was reading Luther's preface to the Epistle to the Romans. About a quarter before nine, while he was describing the change which God works in the heart through faith in Christ, I felt my heart strangely warmed. I felt I did trust in Christ, Christ alone, for salvation: and an assurance was given me that He had taken away my sins, even mine, and saved me from the law of sin and death."

John discovered that brother Charles had received his assurance of salvation a few days previously. The Wesleys were poised to change England by word and song.

But where to begin? John Wesley's first public testimony outside the Fetter Lane Society was in an informal service in a friend's house. With the bluntness that had always been his way he told them that five days before he was not a Christian, and now he was. The lady of the house took grave exception and complained to John's oldest brother Samuel by letter, telling him to put a stop to his brother's madness.

John, meanwhile, had decided to visit the Moravian headquarters in Germany. Before he went, though, he had one important preaching engagement. It was in the University Church of Saint Mary the Virgin, Oxford, at the invitation of the vice-chancellor. There, in front of a congregation of professors, doctors of divinity, and students he nailed his colors to the mast as he preached the sermon that he was to make the cornerstone of the whole future Methodist body of teaching, to be believed and preached by all its ministers: "Salvation by Faith," based on Ephesians 2:8.

That sermon still has power today, 250 years later. A few months ago, a middle-aged man visited our church from out of town. After the service he told me his story. He had been a Methodist all his life, going to church because of duty. Then recently he had started reading Wesley's collection of 44 sermons. As he read "Salvation by Faith," he realized that he had not been born again. Conviction came into his heart, he reached out in faith, trusting Christ only for salvation, and now was a convinced believer with new life flowing through him.

The reaction to that first preaching of the sermon was probably mixed. But once Wesley was back from Germany, he found that churches were shutting their doors one after the other to him. Congregations simply did not like to be told that all their church-going and good works did not make them Christians. Only faith in Christ would do, and faith of a definite kind, arising out of a conviction of sin. It was the exact opposite of the prevailing arid deism so many clergymen preached. Deism, which was a product of the intellectual enlightenment of the time, taught that God had made the universe like a clockmaker makes a clock, wound it up, and left it to run, not intervening any further. It was an awful doctrine, squeezing the life out of real religion. Deism made miracles impossible and prayer useless. No wonder Wesley was unpopular.

Wesley had already experienced something of this closing of pulpits to him, for on Peter Böhler's advice he had been preaching salvation by faith before he himself was converted, and it had not been welcomed. But now he saw the trend intensify. In fact he began to estimate the effectiveness of a sermon according to how much opposition there was to him preaching in the same place again! Not that the shutters slamming on the pulpit steps meant he was underemployed. The religious societies that abounded, who comprised groups of believers who wanted stronger spiritual meat than they got in the parish church, were only too glad to welcome him, and crowds were beginning to flock to hear this small man with the big voice preaching limitless grace.

In any event, the Lord had pulpits enough stored for him that he never imagined: grassy mounds, brick works, market places, quarries, dock-sides, and many other unorthodox platforms. But it nearly didn't happen.

It all came about through an old friend of the Holy Club days, George Whitefield, who had taken his place in Georgia (and had, incidentally, a high regard for the work Wesley had done there). Whitefield had come into his conversion experience some time before and was having a remarkable effect where he preached—and he did preach in odd places. He too was having the experience of closed pulpits; in fact, he had the distinction of being barred from every church in London. At the moment, he was preaching in the open air to the coal miners of Kingswood, near Bristol, 120 miles west of London, and then Britain's second largest city. His first venture in the open air had a congregation of a few hundred. Three weeks later he was preaching to 10,000. But he was due to return to America. So he sent Wesley an urgent Macedonian call to come and help him.

Wesley was not at all sure he should go. The thought of preaching in the open air appalled him. Some random opening of the Bible did not seem to produce the looked-for guidance. Charles was dead against it. In the end, he prayed and drew lots. The method of guidance is not to be recommended, but God overruled: the answer was yes. So, by the skin of his teeth, the greatest traveling open-air evangelist of all time got started.

No doubt apprehensively, he accompanied Whitefield around his circuit of open-air pulpits and saw for himself the crowds that gathered. Next day, Whitefield had gone and it was Wesley's turn to take the plunge.

"At four in the afternoon I submitted to be more vile, and proclaimed in the highways the glad tidings of salvation, speaking from a little eminence in a ground adjoining to the city, to about three thousand people."

The breakthrough had been made—and it was no small thing, for "I could scarce reconcile myself at first to this strange way of preaching in the fields . . . having all my life (till very lately) so tenacious of every point relating to decency and order, that I should have thought the saving of souls almost a sin if it had not been done in a church."

Not that he ever found it natural. He was quite frank where his personal preference lay—and why he took no notice of it.

"I love a commodious room, a soft cushion, a handsome pulpit. But where is my zeal, if I do not trample all these underfoot in order to save one more soul?"

Wesley's willingness to overcome his fleshly preference was amply rewarded. Things began to happen straight away. The rough coal miners and their women folk of Kingswood, for whom no one had ever cared before, responded to the preaching in dramatic ways. People dropped to the ground as though knocked out. Some roared, some wept, some appeared convulsed. But then they came through to peace and joy. Wesley himself was cautious about these phenomena—as he was about any professions of conversion. (He came to believe that a good test was if the convert turned up at the five o'clock prayer meeting the next morning!) As for the Bishop of Bristol, he was aghast. "Sir," he told Wesley, "the pretending to extraordinary revelations of the Holy Ghost is a horrid thing; yes, sir, it is a *very horrid thing*. Sir, you have no business here; you are not commissioned to preach in this diocese: therefore I advise you to go hence."

Wesley was not discouraged. He had already declared to another critic that "the world is my parish." No other concept would do, for God was moving upon the face of the land through this formerly ascetic scholar; it was revival.

The penchant for "method" that had marked Wesley all his life now began to make sense. For it made him tackle the problem of after-care for the converts of the revival in a masterly fashion. Though he was determined to remain a loyal member of the Church of England all his life, yet he knew it was no good handing his converts over to unsympathetic clergy. He built on the religious society idea that had existed for some time, and encouraged the converts to meet together regularly. In the societies, there was a break-down into small groups called classes, and bands, which made personal care much easier. In the band meeting, converts would share their spiritual experiences, give thanks for their blessings, and confess their sins. Members exhorted one another to build up each other's faith. The training of class leaders provided the opportunity for discovering gifts of leadership among ordinary folk that in time would enrich the working classes of Britain. But at the beginning, Wesley's sole aim in founding the classes and bands was to encourage holiness of life, and make people fit for heaven.

When he first preached in the open air at Bristol, Wesley could have had no idea what it would lead to. He lived to be 88 and was traveling almost till the end, which meant 52 years on the roads (such as they were in those days). He described himself as living a "vagabond life," and that was as apt a description as could ever be applied. Some of the statistics and the feats of his traveling are astounding. It is estimated he covered a quarter of a million miles to deliver 40,000 sermons. If he had made an appointment, then he determined to keep it—and keep it on time—whatever the weather or obstacles. He rode through snow, rain, and anything in between; he crossed bogs; he forded rivers. Sometimes he would be riding from five in the morning to eleven at night, with very little break in between. He could cover 50 miles in a day—which is some going on horseback. Once he rode from London to Newcastle on Tyne in six days, covering 280 miles. That would have been a feat in good weather, but in fact he encountered wind, hail, rain, ice, snow, and driving sleet. Sometimes he would hire a carriage. Later in his career he had one of his own, which was equipped as a traveling study. Often, when all other forms of transportation failed, he would walk.

With such incessant traveling, study was a problem. But he learned early on that if he kept his horse on a slack rein, he was able to read without fear that the horse would fall. In fact his testimony was that in all the 52 years of travel, he never had a serious accident, nor was he ever waylaid by that eighteenth-century scourge, the highwayman.

But if there weren't hardships in traveling, there were often plenty waiting for him when he arrived! Not everyone received him as readily as that first crowd at Kingswood. Sometimes the hostility would have been frightening to a lesser man.

Once, in 1743, he was taken by a mob at Walsall, in England's midlands. He was dragged back by the hair when he tried to enter a house, and was propelled from one end of Walsall to the other. When he tried to speak from a doorway, he was shouted down; some cried "Drown him!" some "Hang him!" others "Beat his brains out." One even called out "Crucify him!" Many were for stripping his clothes off, but Wesley said, "That you need not do; I will give you my clothes if you want them."

Wesley was convinced that through all this he was divinely protected. He recalled how many tried to grab hold of his collar to pull him down but could not. Another struck at him from behind with a wooden stick, but the blows were miraculously turned aside. Yet another raised his arm to strike, then let it fall gently on Wesley's hand, saying foolishly, "What soft hair he has!"

Wesley was hustled along, together with his friends. Things were still looking extremely ugly, as the mob carried on shrieking and howling and making their frightening suggestions, when suddenly one of them turned to Wesley and said, "Sir, I will spend my life for you: follow me and not one soul here shall touch a hair of your head." Those who were nearest Wesley now formed themselves into a bodyguard and against the menaces of the rest of the mob escorted Wesley out of the town and down to the river, where his protector put the 120-pound evangelist on his shoulders and carried him across the river to safety.

However, as the years went on, the opposition got less, and places that first met him with a mob now gave him a welcome. By the 1780s even the church pulpits were open to him again, so he had more invitations to preach in them than he could answer.

The scope of Wesley's influence was enormous. Though he never again visited America, Methodism took firm root there through his evangelists Francis Asbury and Dr. Thomas Coke. By any standards, Wesley's was one of the great lives of all time. He influenced not simply the church but a nation. More than one historian has claimed that he saved Britain from a bloody revolution such as engulfed France. And yet he did bring a revolution to many; a revolution of love.

> *Love divine, all loves excelling.*
> *Joy of heaven, to earth come down;*
> *Fix in us thy humble dwelling,*
> *All thy faithful mercies crown.*
> *Jesus, Thou art all compassion,*
> *Pure unbounded love Thou art;*
> *Visit us with Thy salvation,*
> *Enter every trembling heart.*
>
> —Charles Wesley

When he lay on his deathbed, all the anxieties and fears he

had before conversion were nowhere to be found. The calm in the face of death he had witnessed in the Moravians on the *Simmonds* was his. The afternoon before his death, unable to say very much, he cried out, "The best of all is—God is with us!" then lifting his hand repeated, "The best of all is—God is with us!"

During the night the phrase on his lips was, "I'll praise—I'll praise." The next morning at ten, with a calm "Farewell!" he was gone. He had loved so much and served so well.

For further reading: *The Burning Heart,* by A. Skevington Wood (Paternoster Press, England) *Journal,* by John Wesley — many different editions

5

Corrie ten Boom

Quartz watches, with their silent micro-second accuracy, are fine. But they've meant the virtual demise of one endearing species: the old-fashioned watchmaker. To step through the doorways of their shops, bell jangling as you entered, was to enter a different world. As you closed the door, the street noises of haste and feverish activity were on the other side of the glass panel, leaving you with the warm-bath feeling of rest and calm, measured by the tick-tick-tick of a thousand watches, and the tock-tock-tock of as many clocks hanging all around the walls. As for the watchmaker himself, by a strange paradox, this man whose job was time, seemed to have a transcendent timelessness. He would never be hurried, but neither would he ever fall to the sin of procrastination. Courtesy, too, was part of his make-up, built into him by the long traditions of family firms stretching back centuries.

Casper ten Boom of Haarlem, Holland, was the very archetype of this very special breed. Tall, patriarchally bearded as befitted his 80-plus years, he ruled his shop with benign gentleness, not so much imposing standards of excellence as nurturing them like prize fruit trees. The shop, known to all Haarlem as the Beje, was also his house; a crooked, lovable jumble of odd-shaped rooms, asymmetrical floors, added extensions, and improvised alterations that were a fairytale illustrator's delight. If it had been a toy shop, you would have expected Pinocchio to come right out and meet you from behind the counter.

However, it was not the toy shop, but the watchmaker's, and so coming to meet you would have been, if not Papa ten Boom himself, then one of his two daughters, Betsie or Corrie, both around 50 years old. Betsie was the older by seven years, and both were spinsters. If you came in the daytime, you might also meet the employees, Christoffels, an elderly repairman, and Toos, the lady who looked after the accounts. At other times you might find the house full of bubbling, happy people, for Mr. ten Boom had another daughter, Nollie, and a son Willem, both married with families who often visited. Willem perhaps visited less often, for he lived a busy life in Hilversum as a Dutch Reformed minister running a home for elderly people.

It was a happy, contented family. The only shadow that had fallen on them in years was the death of Mrs. ten Boom, but the strong Christian faith that vibrated through them all meant they had no fears about death. Under Papa ten Boom's wise counseling they had a rock-solid trust in the faithfulness of God, who always did what was best for His children. But this staid, solid Dutch family was about to have that faith shaken to its foundations, and be pitched into a true-life adventure they would never have dreamed possible. For this was 1940, and Hitler's jack-booted troops were on the march, trampling peace into the ground right across Europe.

For weeks, if not months, all Holland had been living in uncertainty about the little German with the moustache who had set up the most horrific tyranny Europe had seen since the French Revolution. Would he respect Dutch neutrality, or not? Reassurance from the government helped no one but the most gullible. There was a horrible feeling of inevitability as the war raged around Holland's borders. It was like watching the waves lap around the walls of a sandcastle, knowing that the tide must win in the end.

The end for free Holland was swift when it came. The typical German strategy of a sudden attack without warning, followed by the pouring in of division after division of troops, and in five days it was all over. Holland was now annexed to Hitler's evil empire. German soldiers were everywhere. New laws and new restrictions were imposed, and there was precious little any Dutchman could do about it.

At first, life went on normally. The curfew was a nuisance, but on the whole people moved around, shopped, and worked as they had done before. In fact the ten Boom family even found their business increased as the young soldiers of the occupation bought souvenirs and gifts for their girlfriends back home. But then the brutality of satanic Nazism began to make itself felt, and no community felt it more than the Jews, of whom there were a great many in Holland. The ten Boom family, who had always held a special place in their hearts for the descendants of God's own people of Israel, watched in shocked dismay as they saw Jewish stores openly looted and defaced, Jewish people humiliated in the streets. Every Jewish man, woman and child was marked for special abuse by a yellow cloth Star of David which they were forced to sew on their garments. But as dreadful as it was to see this treatment, it was worse to realize that individual Jews, indeed whole Jewish families, were simply disappearing.

With their love for the Lord, and their love for His special people, it was only a matter of time before the ten Booms would help in some way. At first, it was quite small (though still risky); things like giving room for a Jewish rabbi's books before he was taken away, or helping a Jewish fellow-watchmaker whose home was raided. But news of their kindness spread among the Jewish community, and one night the family heard a ring at their bell and went out to find a petrified lady pleading for shelter. They took her in. Two nights later, an elderly couple were on their doorstep with the same report.

It was then that Corrie discovered her brother Willem had been operating in the Dutch resistance movement for some time, and his nursing home had been a base for helping Jews escape Nazi clutches. Corrie and the others drew on his experience.

"You'll need ration cards if you're to feed them," he said.

"How?" Corrie asked innocently.

"They'll have to be stolen," replied the respectable Dutch Reformed minister coolly. Corrie gulped. She had been brought up never to do such things. Yet this war had already forced on her the telling of a lie, when the Nazi officer had asked her if she had a radio set, and she had replied no.

So Corrie went on her first "underground" expedition, with much prayer and a racing heart. By a wonderful sequence of events, she found herself able to contact a sympathetic worker in the food office who organized a hold-up of himself. It cost him a couple of black eyes and cut lip, for his friends had to make it authentic! But Corrie ended up with a hundred ration cards, for the Lord was making it plain that their present three guests were going to be far from the last. Indeed, as these first refugees were moved on to safer accommodations, their places were quickly taken by others, and theirs by others, and theirs by yet more. It seemed endless, as the ten Boom home became a secret transit camp for Jew after Jew. And all the time the ten Booms managed to keep up some semblance of "business as usual," especially when the customers were German soldiers. Resistance workers covered their movements, calling ostensibly to get a watch repaired or to read the electricity meter.

One night, Corrie found herself being taken on a mysterious bike ride by her nephew Kik across the bumpy cobbled streets. Clattering along on the cloth-bound wheels (tires had disintegrated long ago) she wondered where on earth they could be going. To her surprise, she was ushered into the large house of one of their most wealthy customers whom she knew well, a large fat man she always called Pickwick, because he was so like the Dickensian character. But he had not sent for her to repair his clock. It turned out he was heading up the resistance work in the area. Others were in the room, and Corrie was introduced. All of them, it seemed, were called "Smit"! The ten Boom's work with the Jews was now so important that it was vital certain steps were taken. She was told of the help that was available: false identity papers, secret transport arrangements, and so on. But most crucial of all, there must be a secret room in the Beje. Otherwise, when there was a search by the police, as there must be sooner or later, there would be no hope for anyone in the house. Corrie's head spun. It seemed so unreal. This was the stuff of the movies. And yet it *was* real. Here was a distinguished, courteous man talking to her now, promising to come around and see to it.

True to his word, the man came. Papa ten Boom, somewhat baffled by the drama of events (as far as he was concerned, he was only doing the simple, obvious, and necessary thing of helping God's people) let him get on with dashing all over the house with his tape measure. The man made approving noises as he saw just how odd and jumbled the tall, quaint house was.

Slightly breathless, "Mr. Smit" climbed to the very top room of all, Corrie's bedroom, and breathed out what breath he had left in scarcely controlled excitement.

"Absolutely perfect! If I build a brick partition here, I can make it so all the Gestapo in Germany couldn't find it!" Then seeing Corrie's slightly disconcerted face, he smiled, and went on, "Don't worry. You will still have room to sleep."

Over the next few weeks the shop had a lot more "customers" than usual, coming nonchalantly through the door. None stayed too long to arouse suspicion, yet miraculously, a wall went up. It was plastered and painted to look as old as the room, and lo and behold, Corrie found herself in a bedroom she could hardly realize was any different to what it had been all her life. And yet she knew that by the end of the bed was a panel, and when that panel was lifted there was a way through to a space two feet, six inches wide and the length of the room. Corrie tried crawling through. Yes, she, the lady with middle-age spread, could manage it okay. "Let's hope our Jews will be thinner than me," she puffed as she straightened up.

Another "Mr. Smit" got their telephone reconnected (ordinary Hollanders by this time had all had their telephones cut off.)

Meanwhile, the Beje was becoming something of a permanent home for some Jews. These were the ones who could not be placed elsewhere because of special risks. There was Eusie, as Corrie named him, a cultured Jew with a wry sense of humor and a love for the faith of his fathers. Papa ten Boom loved to hear Eusie read from the Old Testament. Henk, a young lawyer, joined him. Then there was Leendert, a schoolteacher, who arranged an alarm system so that in the event of a "visit," the illegal residents would have time to reach the hiding place. They all had great fun practicing drills, ringing the alarm at unexpected times so that they perfected the art of getting everyone up to the hiding place in under two minutes, leaving the living room as though for all the world no more than Papa, Betsie, and Corrie alone had been there for hours on end. It took some doing; not only did they have to make the physically exhausting climb up the twisty staircase, but they had to whip away ashtrays, meal plates, odd clothes, and anything else that gave the tell-tale sign that the ten Booms had had a guest. Corrie herself had to be trained to be able to deny all knowledge of Jews convincingly when rudely woken with a torch shining in her eyes.

The main problem they knew would by Mary Itallie, for Mary was 70 years old, and asthmatic. But no one was willing to safeguard their own safety by turning her out. Two other ladies, and the ten Booms' young apprentice, completed the group.

This strange community, thrown together by the tragedy of war, developed a creative and fulfilling life together. They had concerts, they read plays (sometimes by the light of Corrie's bike), and Betsie succeeded in doing the most amazing things with the limited food that was available. And there were the Bible readings from the big, brass-bound Bible. The ten Booms made no attempt to force their Christian beliefs on their guests. In fact, they honored the Judaism that had come into their home. When Christmas came, they celebrated Hanukkah too, and entered into their friends' celebrations with joy and enthusiasm. But neither did the ten Booms hide their belief in Jesus Christ, the Messiah. There was a precious harmony in the home. It could have gone on till the end of the war. If only . . .

For all the laughter and enjoyment in the cramped confined conditions of the Beje, Corrie was getting increasingly worried. They had had one or two narrow squeaks, and to her dismay she found that quite unexpected people were aware of their work. If, for all the secrecy, their fame was spreading, surely it could only be a matter of time before somebody not on their side heard. But she must go on working, committing everything to the Lord, for it was His work, and He had guided them so much up to now. Yet perhaps the time would come when that alarm would sound, not for a practice, but for real.

When it did, Corrie was sick with the flu. The first time she was aware of what was happening was when she woke with the buzzer penetrating the cotton-wool stuffiness of her head and saw the blurry shapes passing her bed one by one, fear vibrating from them in waves. Corrie struggled to come to, rolled out of bed, slid the panel behind the last trembling figure, got back into bed, and tried to look and sound as normal as she could when the door was flung open and the officer barked out, "You—what's your name?"

Her reply brought a mixture of satisfaction and scorn to the officer's voice.

"Ha! The ringleader! Get up. Dress. At once."

While Corrie struggled to obey, all the time breathing silent prayers for this moment she had dreaded so much, the officer demanded, "Where have you hidden the Jews?" Corrie was thankful for her training.

"Jews? I don't know anything about Jews." (*O Lord,* thought Corrie, *please forgive me for these lies!*)

She dressed as quickly as she could, not to please him, but to get him away from the room with all possible haste.

Downstairs there followed the worst moments of her life so far—though could she but know it, worse were to come in the months ahead. Father, Betsie, and Toos were there looking brave but strained. It was obvious from the pile of silver on the table the soldiers had already started searching the house. Could the hiding place survive such a thorough and systematic probing?

Pushed into the back room away from the rest of her family, Corrie was commanded once again to reveal the location of the Jews. Again she denied all knowledge. Then the officer, brutalized by the evil cause he served and the inhuman philosophy it taught, began to hit this 50-year-old gentle spinster about the face. Almost losing consciousness, she called out to the Lord for protection. This seemed to anger the man even more, but even so, he stopped. His next step gave Corrie more pain; it was to take her back into the front room and exchange her for Betsie. When Betsie returned, her mouth was bleeding, her face bruised. But still the officer was denied the information he demanded.

Above them, they could hear the sound of splintering wood. The place was being torn apart. How long before that room was discovered? The situation was getting worse all the time. Their signal to warn visitors when they were being raided had been discovered by the eagle-eyed officer; friends were calling, only to fall unwittingly right into the trap and be arrested. Then the phone rang to the surprise of the officers. Now they knew for sure they had come to the nerve-center of the resistance operation! But the location of the hiding place still baffled them. At last the soldiers had to give up; but the officer refused to believe he was wrong.

"We'll starve them out. We'll guard the place until the very stink of their rotting corpses tells us where they are. Now—all of you. Get moving."

The next hours were filled with heartbreak. Herded into the gym of the police station, all the formalities of registering the new prisoners were gone through, and then followed the journey to the Gestapo Headquarters in the Hague. Corrie soon found that not only she and Betsie and Papa had been rounded up, but Willem and Nollie too. Yes, and there was Pickwick, his head bleeding, bruised, but unbowed from the interrogation he had received. Papa was given the option of release if he would promise not to be involved in such activities again. Unhesitatingly he replied, "If I return to my house, I will open my door to anyone in need."

Papa was not released. Corrie was to discover much later that 10 days after, he was dead, a victim of the rigors of prison life.

The next stage was the prison at Schevenigen. Separated now from the rest of her family, Corrie found herself thrown into a tiny cell with four others. Corrie could hardly breathe for the stench. There was but one cot; the other prisoners had to make do with straw mattresses on the floor. Her flu was making her extremely feverish. She felt so ill. When food was shoved through the hatch, she could not touch it. For days she was like that. She struggled to eat and to keep going. Her companions occupied themselves in various ways. One would pace up and down the mere six paces that were possible in that cramped space. Another would play cards she had manufactured out of toilet paper.

After two weeks, still feeling ill, Corrie was summoned out of her cell. Was this release? In fact, it was to go to the doctor, who examined her and found she had pleurisy, a lung infection. It seemed as though there might be something better than that horrible, crowded cell; surely the prison hospital could be no worse and might be a good deal better?

In fact, the authorities' answer to the problem of a contagious, ill prisoner was simple: isolate her in solitary confinement. Her transfer to solitary was not explained to her as being for a medical reason, however. She had no idea why she was there. All she knew was that all the restrictions of the dehumanizing punishment were imposed with full rigor. She was not even allowed to sing a birthday song to herself. Her one solace was that she had managed to smuggle in a gospel booklet. It was her lifeline from God. She would read it till the ache of loneliness flew and the warmth of God's love enveloped her. Her only other fellowship was with the ants that popped up through a crack in the floor. She developed quite a relationship with them!

In spite of the abysmal conditions and the total lack of medical aid, Corrie gradually recovered her strength. Also spring began to penetrate even this most dismal of cells. She could look out of the tiny barred window and feel the sunshine on her face. Two other events cheered her enormously. The first was when, in a rare moment of prison slackness, messages got through the cell network with the news that with the exception of her and Betsie, all the others captured that dreadful night had been released. The second was when a parcel arrived from the released Nollie herself. Apart from the blessings of the food and vitamins she had sent, there was a secret message hidden under the stamp. It said: *All the watches in your closet are safe.* Corrie had no doubt what Nollie was saying: All our Jews got away! Praise the Lord! God *was* in control!

"March! At the double." The officer rasped out his order, his voice as chill as the morning air that turned his breath into ghostly palls of steam. Corrie took hold of Betsie's arm to help her along. The two sisters had been reunited for some weeks since Corrie's solitary confinement at Schevenigen. Since then they had been placed in a camp in Vught, where they had been put to work making radios for the Luftwaffe; they made sure as few of the sets as possible worked. But now where were they off to? On the one hand, they had the hope that the move meant the Allies were getting close and perhaps the war might soon be over; on the other, they feared what the Germans might do now that the tide was running against them. Yesterday, the women had listened with helpless horror while in the men's camp names had been called on the loudspeaker, to be followed by shot after shot as 700 men were disposed of.

After an age of stumbling and marching urged on by the shouting guards, the straggling hundreds of disheveled, weary, weak women arrived at a railway siding, to see standing there a line of open-topped freight cars. Brutally, the women were forced to clamber up and over the high sides to be piled 80 to a car. Half that would have crowded them: After a few hours of this stifling misery, the train started with a jerk, but no one fell, for no one could. The appalling, torturous journey went on for mile after mile for two days. Occasional stops brought water to the lucky few near the sides, and hard, unpalatable bread was passed around, but few could eat in the awful, unsanitary conditions. Corrie looked after her older and weaker sister as best she could, but there was little anyone could do to relieve the dreadful pressure of stinking body pressed against stinking body.

At last the nightmare journey ended, and the thirsty, hungry women were hauled out. At last they breathed fresh air and drank clean water. But soon the respite was over. It was back to marching, and the pathetic column stumbled its way until the leading women saw a complex of gray buildings surrounded by a high barbed-wire fence, its continuous line throwing up at intervals tall towers. Inside the circle of towers there was one building with a smokestack rivaling them for height, with a gray plume sluggishly rising, darkened by ash-flakes. A gasp of horror spread back along the ragged ranks. A concentration camp! And those who knew whispered the dread name. Ravensbruck! The infamy of the place was already part of the ghastly folklore of World War II. Corrie felt her heart thumping in dread. But something else was beating against her body: a Bible, in a string bag around her neck under her thin prison dress. Nollie had managed to smuggle one to her and to Betsie on the single visit she had been permitted at Vught. That book would be her guide and strength whatever lay ahead—provided she could keep it!

Their first experiences of the camp were daunting enough. Two nights they were kept out in the open in rain and cold, and it looked as though they would be kept out a third when they were suddenly hustled off to be registered.

Registration became a huge test of faith for the two ten Booms. In the first place, these modest, godly, middle-aged spinsters were, with the others, required to strip totally naked and parade down past the leering eyes of the male guards. Corrie realized in a fresh way part of the shame of Jesus, who, though Christian art usually avoids the fact out of reverence, was crucified in that same state. But worse than the shame for Corrie was the realization that there would be no chance of getting the precious Bible past those guards, nor the vitamin drops which she believed were essential to keep Betsie alive. But she prayed and trusted God to help her. A desperate plea to take Betsie to the toilets caused her unexpectedly to be allowed in the shower room before the others. She quickly hid the articles in some old benches, near where their new prison dresses with their big stitched *X*s were waiting, and then back out to the line. Through the ordeal of the gauntlet of the prying eyes, soothed to a degree by having the fresh, if cold, shower, Corrie made her way to the dresses. She took the largest she could find that wouldn't look too ridiculous, and deftly put the little bag around her neck. Feeling as conspicuous as a pumpkin in an onion patch, she walked on. She saw to her dismay that every prisoner was being searched by SS men running their hands all over them. But for some reason, the guards missed her. God was the God of miracles, even in Ravensbruck.

By now, it was the early hours of the morning, so when she and Betsie were taken into their barracks, they found the bed they were piled into already occupied by three women. But they soon found those were not the only occupants. "Ouch!" In spite of all the pain she had suffered from beatings and deprivations, the little pin-prick still made Corrie jump. And again. And again.

"Betsie!" Corrie hissed. "Fleas! Hundreds of them!" But Betsie had already found them for herself—or rather, they had found her. But Corrie thought Betsie's flea philosophy hard to take. "Thank God for the fleas, Corrie. The Bible says we must thank Him for everything."

At 4:30 A.M. they found themselves outside once again.

That, they discovered, was regular roll-call time at Ravensbruck. Their day was spent in the most difficult work. It made the radio assembly at Vught seem like leisure. Here, they were digging or pushing heavy rollers. It was altogether too much for the weak Betsie. Unable to lift a shovelful of dirt, she lifted what she could. A pitiless guard saw the little clod on Betsie's spade and smashed her club in derisive scorn across the poor woman, making blood run.

Instinctively, Corrie grabbed her shovel and ran after the guard, whose back was now turned to her. The bleeding Betsie threw herself in front.

"Corrie! No! There must be no hate." Corrie looked at her pitiful sister. She saw that her appeal to her was not based on fear of the consequence, but true, forgiving love for her oppressor.

As the days went on, the two sisters found a change coming over their overcrowded flea ridden barracks. There was less anger; bitterness became diluted. They knew why. As they tried to establish a Christian witness in the precious and sparse off-duty hours, with services that included people of all denominations or none, so there were many who were finding out for the first time just what it meant to know Jesus as Saviour. How many found peace with God in that horrible room with its three tiers of bunks, its square yards of emaciated human bodies, can never be known on this earth. But they were many. That precious Bible became the means of life to more and more. And the two sisters made a discovery; the fleas for which Betsie had insisted they thank God were their allies after all. It was because of them that the guards kept out of their barracks, and left them in peace to hold the services.

Corrie and Betsie also found their own closeness becoming increasingly precious. They would talk about the future. Betsie was quite definite. She had had a "vision."

"Corrie, when this is over we've got to help all those who have suffered. There will be many crippled minds to be healed. God has shown me a house, a big house in beautiful grounds. The house has tall windows, and statues in recesses. Oh, and there's a grand, sweeping staircase. All those poor, torn, minds will find healing there. They'll be helped by the garden, growing beautiful things. And then, when we've done that, we'll travel the world and tell people that love is stronger than hate, and no pit so deep that God is not deeper still. It will be soon, Corrie. By the new year, we both will be free. I know—God has shown me."

Betsie *was* free by the new year. Not to go back to Holland, but to that greatest of all liberties. She had been weak throughout her incarceration, but taking their relentless toll were the malnutrition, the heavy labor, and the lack of proper care (though miraculously Corrie's vitamin drops kept going until the very day a new supply was smuggled in). She became so ill, even the heartless overseers had to admit she was a hospital case, and so she was admitted to the sick bay. Corrie managed to get in some surreptitious visits. She could see her dear sister was getting weaker, and after a short time she died. Sad as Corrie was, she was thankful that Betsie was spared these dreadful roll calls, the hours they spent on the barrack square in the freezing cold, and the awful grind of the daily labor, though both had lately been put on indoor work. Yes, Betsie was free, truly free. But what about herself, and what about Betsie's vision?

Three days after Betsie's death, with total unexpectedness, Corrie had a summons to the administration office. She could hardly believe her ears as the magic word was spoken.

Entlassen—released. A paper was stamped with the same word. Corrie's heart leapt with joy. It seemed too good to be true—and so it was, at least for a time. A medical check found her too ill to be released. It was ironic to reflect that she had been considered fit enough to undertake the ardors of concentration camp life, but not fit enough to go into the outside world. Anxious days and weeks in hospital followed, but at last, that precious piece of paper delivered what it promised. *Entlassen.*

When she got back to Holland, after a somewhat perilous journey having to dodge the allied bombers as well as marauding Germans, she found her homeland still under enemy occupation. Her homecoming was nevertheless a thrilling, emotional time, and there was not long to wait before the Dutch liberation. She began speaking in various churches about her experiences, and Betsie's vision. One day, a lady came to her and said she would like to offer her house for the work of rehabilitating the victims of the war. When Corrie saw the house she raised her heart in praise to God. There were the tall windows; the recessed statues; the broad, sweeping staircase; and the beautiful, beautiful gardens. To that house over the next decade and a half came those who had only known the harshness of prison and camp life. They found peace, healing—and Jesus.

Once the work was going, and in capable hands, Corrie knew she must carry out the second part of Betsie's vision: the world must know how love had conquered hate in that most inhospitable of environments, a Nazi concentration camp. She believed God told her to start in America, so, with the simple faith she had learned in her years of peril, she drew out her savings, and having only the barest of contacts to begin with, she set out, an old maid of retirement age who should have been thinking about settling down somewhere in a quiet bungalow by the sea. It was the beginning of a new career as a traveling evangelist that was to take her in the next 30 years to 64 countries. She became, as she put it, "a tramp for the Lord." Nor did she restrict herself to comfortable church groups. With a special love for those in prison, having suffered so much herself and found the power not only to survive without bitterness, but, much more, to forgive her very tormentors, including the man who had betrayed her at the beginning, she deliberately sought out congregations of the toughest and roughest. Once, in the Philippines, she spoke to the jail's most notorious criminals with such effect that some called the conversions, prayer meetings, and Bible study groups that followed her preaching "revival."

Her fame spread through books she wrote and books written about her, and especially through the film of her life, "The Hiding Place." But she never lost her ability to communicate with ordinary people. She operated on what she called the "KISS" principle: Keep It Simple, Stupid!

She died on April 15, 1983, her ninety-first birthday. The closing hymn at her memorial service expressed the valiant conviction of the lady who refused to accept that a quiet, middle-aged spinster was powerless against the evil anti-Semitism defacing her world. In heaven she was probably singing along with her friends as they sent the triumphant stanzas ringing through the chapel:

Stand up, stand up for Jesus, the strife will not be long;
This day the noise of battle, the next the victor's song.

—*George Duffield*

For further reading: *The Hiding Place,* by Corrie ten Boom (Hodder & Stoughton)
Corrie ten Boom: Her Life, Her Faith, by Carole C. Carlson (Revell)

Cecil Phillips

The last dying gasp of the diesel engine and a final shudder of the vibrating windows gave notice that the double-decker bus had reached the end of its run.

"Filwood Broadway, Knowle West. This is it."

As I stepped off the platform and put my foot on the pavement that summer Sunday in 1958, I felt like Columbus beaching his boat on the American shore. Although I had lived most of my life in the city of Bristol, this district was a whole new world to me. I had never had cause to visit there before, nor did I have any particular wish to visit. Why should

I? It was hardly one of the tourist attractions of ancient England. Thrown up in a rash of red-brick building frenzy before and after World War II, it had become, as far as some people were concerned, the dumping ground for all the problem families who couldn't be housed anywhere else—"The dustbin of Bristol," one newspaper had called it.

Actually, it didn't look that bad as I took in my first glance. I could see where the idealistic planners had got things off to a good start with the long, straight boulevard of the Broadway, divided in the middle by a grassed strip, and a semicircle of more grass at its far end. But the urgencies of the effects of wartime bombing and slum-clearance meant that the repetitive rows of dwellings had spread like spilled oil across more and more land to defeat the original grand design of tree-lined spacious streets.

But I hadn't come to see the view but to meet the girl who was walking toward me. Pat worked in my office, and I'd been flattered when she had asked *me* out: true, it had been to come to church, which wasn't particularly where I would have wanted to go, but it was a start.

We walked to the top of the Broadway to the half-circle of grass, and into the building that lay behind, identified by the lettering above the doorway as the Filwood Community Centre. She piloted me through the door and into a room that looked like a school classroom. A group of 20 or so young people were just about to start their service, led by a man at the front, square, thickset. I guessed he was about 50 years old, his slightly graying dark hair, though short, flopping about over his forehead, a tooth missing. When he spoke, he had a Bristol accent as thick as the city's Avon mud. Brought up as I had been in the respectable Church of England, I wasn't really prepared for the sheer informality of his approach.

"Keith's going to teach us a chorus," he said. Teenage son Keith hauled out to the front a record player and produced a Tennessee Ernie LP. After getting set up we were ready to go.

If, when you give the best of your service,
Telling the world that the Saviour is come,
Be not dismayed if men do not believe you,
He'll understand, and say "Well done!"

I was fascinated, and when this broad man spoke, sincerity shone through.

The next week I returned, and after the service went to his home around the corner from the "church." The warmth of the room when I entered wasn't due to the summer sun. It was sheer love and joy radiating from Cecil Phillips, his wife, Edna, and the young people packing the little sitting room. I went home that night and told my mother, "I think for the first time in my life I have found real Christianity." It was an obvious overstatement; but it was a true reflection of the impact this remarkable man had on me. And yet, to use the word "remarkable" almost defeats the object of telling his story. For the most impressive thing is that he was an *ordinary* man; not just in his blue-collar, working class background, but in his Christian service. There was no sudden great burden from God such as Glady's Aylward had for China; there was no climactic realization of destiny as William Booth experienced; nor was there a dramatic crisis calling for extraordinary actions as with Corrie ten Boom. Cecil simply did what seemed the next obvious thing to do. The work he did never grew to world proportions, attracting fame. He died, as he lived, in obscurity. But for that very reason, he may be a bigger challenge to our Christian coziness. For most of us also count ourselves "ordinary."

Cecil knew hardship from his earliest days. Born July 19, 1913, his father, a Bristol railwayman, had a hard job providing for a family of five boys and four girls. Sometimes Cecil came downstairs at six-thirty in the morning to find his mother sewing; she had stayed up all night patching and sewing to keep her family clothed.

But what Mum and Dad Phillips could not provide materially was more than made up by the spiritual wealth they passed on to their children. Their's was a practical, straightforward Christianity. From his father, Cecil learned what it was to live in absolute honesty. Cecil remembered how, when he had started work, his father would not allow him to bring home from the factory one tiny little thing needed for a job at home. Dad Phillips also taught Cecil the value of common sense, treating with scorn the false spirituality that said "The Lord this" and "The Lord that" when the plain and obvious was staring them in the face.

From his mother, Cecil learned the realities of "love your neighbor as yourself." Those who called at dinner time inevitably had a meal in front of them. It was only later that Cecil realized the meal came from her own plate.

In fact, from them both, Cecil came to value plain, practical Christianity. "Faith without works is dead" was always one of his key texts. He remembered all his life how one day he was walking with his father, when suddenly, it seemed from nowhere, a man they knew to be mentally sick came charging down the street, shirt torn, blood flowing from his face. Without hesitation, Dad Phillips ran to him, put his arm around him, and calmed him.

Impressive as his parents' example was, Cecil did not become a Christian while he lived with them. He saw not just their lives but the lives of their fellow chapel-goers, and to the judgmental eye of the growing teenager they didn't seem to measure up. Sunday only Christianity, with no demonstration of transformed lives during the week nauseated him. He decided it was not for him. So when Cecil was old enough to say no to his parents, he broke his chapel links, and that was how it remained for years to come. He became a pipe-bender in a metal tube factory and set about earning enough to wed

the girl of his dreams, Edna, with whom he had fallen irretriev-
ably in love. In time, they married, and set up home in a nice
area of the city, had two children, Keith and Patricia, and
seemed to have a typical life of respectable, non-militant
paganism.

But at the tube factory there was a thorn in the flesh. A
young apprentice who simply would not shut up about religion. He was always going on about "being saved." It drove
Cecil crazy. In the end, perhaps to keep the nuisance quiet, he
allowed himself to be enticed into a visit to an evangelistic
meeting at the very chapel he had left 17 years before. As he
listened to the preacher expounding the ageless message, "Ye
must be born again," he felt things stirring in him he could
not quiet. By the time he got home afterwards, he was sure
God had been speaking to him. The thing must be settled
that night. Too proud to go to his parents or his Christian
brother, he decided to seek help from a local Congregational
minister. Cecil left the man's house shaking his head, no wiser
than before. There was nothing to do but to swallow his pride
and go to brother Frank. There, as midnight approached,
Frank explained the gospel, and Cecil, at the age of 31,
became a new creature in Christ Jesus as he knelt and asked
God's forgiveness and invited the Saviour into his life.

Edna could not quite tell what it was all about. It was all
new to her; unlike Cecil, she had never heard the gospel
explained in her childhood. She adopted a "wait and see"
approach. As for Keith and Patricia, their ages of six and two
meant they were unaware of anything different.

It was at work that Cecil's "new birth" made the biggest
impact. Though he never forced his new faith on his workmates, neither did he make any secret of it, and so he got the
ribbing and downright scorn that are part of the price of confessing Christ openly.

The very first day at work he made his new faith plain, and
a week later, with knees knocking, he took part in an open-air

meeting right outside the factory gates after work. A woman from the factory came up to him as he sang with the rest and said in her burred Bristol dialect, "What bist thee doin' 'ere? Thee makes enough row during the day." Cecil wished the ground would swallow him up. But he kept going. He saw it as a test.

He said later, "I believe the Lord gives a test before He gives us important tasks to do. If we do not come through, then he does not give us the work."

Cecil's newfound faith began to make itself felt at home as well. Edna did not mind her husband's conversion, but she held herself detached. She had been brought up in an undemanding church that never seemed to make eternal issues seem all that important, certainly not so that they would actually affect your life and alter your timetable as they seemed to be doing to Cecil right now. Whereas Sundays had been the time for getting the garden straight, now Cecil was striding the two miles each way it took to get to church. Even more, he was going weekdays too! Surely that was going a bit far, the bemused Edna wondered. And rain or snow didn't seem to make any difference to him either. Even in the house he was different. He made time each day to pray and read the Bible; did normal working men do such things?

Still she resisted the pleas from Cecil to go with him.

"I've got too much to do," she would say. Or, "I can't leave the children on their own." She tried that excuse once too often. Cecil smiled his little crooked grin that always showed when he had a trump card up his sleeve.

"I've been to old Mrs. Smith across the road, and she says she'll baby-sit for us tonight." There was no way out. So Edna went, and though nothing dramatic happened that night, she kept on going, and gradually the truths of sin and salvation sank in until she could also say, "I know."

Life looked good for the Phillips family. Materially, they were making their way. Cecil had a secure job, a house becoming more and more theirs as they payed off the mortgage, and now and again a little bit extra to save. Domestically, they had a happy home, two lovely young children, and plenty to fill their days. Best of all, spiritually, they were united in Christ, sharing now not only the love of their hearts for each other, but love for God too.

So it seemed to Cecil one day at work as whistling cheerfully to himself unheard among the metallic noises of drills, saws, and hammers around him making all manner of utilitarian sculptures of piping, he climbed a ladder to the framework 25 feet up where lengths of tube were stored. He reached across to select the piece he wanted, when suddenly in an awful moment his foot slipped and he hurtled to the hard floor below, his stocky frame crashing on to it with a jarring thud. Instantly he was surrounded by workmates. They found Cecil barely conscious, his face contorting in a thousand different folds as pain spasms tunnelled through his nerve fibers mercilessly. A wash of sound flowed over him, voices merging into each other.

"Cecil, are you all right?" Silly question! "'E's 'urt bad—ring fur an ambulance .... Let 'im lie still ... mustn't move 'im ...."

The broad Bristol accents tumbled into his ears, but all Cecil could do was moan. The pain was excruciating. But he was conscious of Ron, a young apprentice he had led to the Lord not long before. Unashamedly in front of the men Ron was praying.

At last the ambulance came, and the expert hands of the ambulance men got Cecil into the vehicle and then into the hospital with the minimum of suffering.

Eventually, Cecil found a doctor at the end of the bed giving his verdict.

"You're lucky to be alive, in fact pretty lucky not to be paralyzed. But I'm sorry your back is badly damaged. We're going to have to operate. After, you're going to wear a plaster cast for quite a time to come, and you'll probably have to wear some kind of surgical corset all your life."

Cecil's thoughts immediately centered on one thing.

"Doctor, what about my work?"

The doctor pursed his lips, trying to make things sound as good as he could.

"Oh, you'll work again all right, but I think you'll have to look for something a bit lighter."

"Something a bit lighter" turned out to be caretaker at the local Masonic Hall. The advantage of the job was there was an apartment on the premises to live in. Losing his comparatively well-paid work as a pipe-bender had meant he couldn't afford the family house any longer, and had to give it up. Still, he made the best of things he could while he waited for the summons to hospital for the operation.

While he morosely considered his problems, one day his thoughts were interrupted by an urgent knocking on the door. Edna went to answer, and came back into the room white-faced.

"Cec, I've got to go, quick!" she shouted as she pulled on a coat. "Our Keith's fallen into a bombed site and hurt himself."

Cecil, unable to move fast enough, stayed helpless in the house, worrying and praying. A neighbor came in after a while to give the news that Edna had gone with Keith to the hospital. When Edna at last returned, she was alone and met Cecil's anxious, questioning gaze. "They're keeping him in. He's broken his thigh and his arm."

Cecil buried his head in his hands. First him, now his son. Who next? Lord, what are you doing?

A few days later, there was another urgent knock on the door. Another rapid putting on of her coat and Edna scurrying out. Daughter Tricia, playing in a friend's house, had pulled a kettle of boiling water over herself and suffered a bad scalding. She had been taken into the burn unit at the hospital.

A little later, Cecil was in a hospital bed himself, waiting for his orthopedic surgery. Abrasive Joblike thoughts raced through his mind, rubbing away at his faith.

"Why does God do this? I've lost my health, my job, and my home, and now all my family, bar Edna, is in hospital. Is God a God of love?"

There was no voice from heaven giving the answer. Cecil simply had to cling on in naked faith, thrusting out his long jaw in defiance of the circumstances that others would have called bad luck. It was only later that he found he could point to a Bible text that satisfied his questions: "all things work together for good to them that love God" (Rom. 8:28, *KJV*).

But before that realization could dawn, worse was to come. The operation left him unable to do the caretaking job because he could no longer shovel coal for the boiler. No job meant no accommodation. The only avenue left open was to apply to the city council to be housed by them. There were a number of council housing estates around Bristol. As he swallowed his pride to fill in the application forms, Cecil accepted his lot with as good grace as he could muster, and made only one condition. "Anywhere except Knowle West: I wouldn't go to that dump for all the money in the world!"

The Phillipses had heard reports about this large development on the southern outskirts of Bristol. There were stories about the residents being so ignorant, dirty, or both, that they kept their house-coal in the bath tub. School teachers talked of walking up and down the rows of desks and seeing the lice crawling in children's hair. In actual fact, as the Phillipses were to find out, many of the stories were plain exaggeration, if not downright lies. But it *was* a fact that there were a lot of problem families there, as well as decent ordinary folk who never merited the slanderous comments people who should know better made about them. Prejudice seems to be built into the very genes that make humans human.

Certainly Cecil had his share of prejudice, and when the

envelope went "plop" on the mat, and he found that he and his family had been allocated 45 Connaught Road, Knowle West, he nearly hit the roof. Was God being spiteful or what?

It was Edna who persuaded him to go and at least look. They went, and though the monotonous streets looked ready-made for breeding suicidal depression, the house itself seemed pleasing enough. Neatly small, with one multi-purpose room and a kitchen downstairs, and three bedrooms up, plus bathroom and a garden, there was nothing that really could be said against it apart from the dreaded location. And even that didn't seem quite so bad as Cecil walked down the street and saw the children. Children playing on the pavements, children running across the road, children swinging around lampposts, children in doorways, children in gardens, a laughing, chattering, not-to-say swearing aggregate of children distributed throughout the estate like currants in a cake. And Cecil liked children. Not that he planned to do anything about them, but it was nice to think of Keith and Tricia growing up with plenty of friends.

So the family moved their few sticks of furniture in and started their new life trying to make ends meet on their little bit of welfare money.

Cecil's back was still too bad after the operation to make his way to his church, a couple of miles from their new home. No car rides were available either.

"Let's have our own service right here, just our family," suggested Cecil. It seemed fun to the kids, and Edna was quite happy, so each Sunday the family sat around the dining room table. Cecil would open his Bible, read a passage, and then, what the children liked best of all, he would make it live for them as he put it into his own Bristolese words. They thought their Dad was wonderful.

"Dad," Keith asked, "can I bring a friend on Sunday?"

"And can I?" Tricia chipped in.

"Well, if you like," Cecil said, taken a bit by surprise. "Let 'em all come. Might as well have the neighborhood in," he added with a grin.

And they did. Sunday by Sunday the numbers grew who wanted to hear Mr. Phillips, as they always respectfully called him, tell in his inimitable way how Jonah was swallowed by a whale, or how Noah and Mrs. Noah avoided death by drowning. And it wasn't just the stories. There was the singing too. In those unsophisticated days, to have a lusty chorus was nowhere near such a self-conscious exercise as it became later. "Wide, Wide as the Ocean" and "Away Far Beyond Jordan" became the hit songs of the estate. There was no musical instrument. Pitching the right note was entirely dependent on Edna's voice.

By the end of the year, 50 youngsters were cramming into the Phillipses' living room and kitchen, and spilling into the passageway. Cecil would have to speak from a mid-point in a doorframe between the two halves of the "congregation." Edna learned the hard way Saint Paul's words that love must "bear all things," as she saw this kids' army trample all over her furniture. Rainy days were quite a challenge. There were 50 heads to be dried before they made damp patches on the wallpaper and 100 shoes and boots to be wiped before the carpet took on a brown design the manufacturers never intended. And always, there was the pre-service check that everyone had been to the bathroom. To leave it was to invite chaos once the meeting started.

Where to sit was an obvious problem. It was a case of "first come, first served" for the three pieces of living room furniture and the dining chairs. The next arrivals sat on the table, and everyone else sat on the floor, squashed tightly together into a slab of young humanity. The heat generated was intense, strangely worse in winter than in summer, with the fire, however low it was kept, threatening to melt them like toffee on the stove. As the kids wriggled and squirmed to ease their cramped limbs, shouts punctuated Cecil's story.

"Yere, take yer feet outa my back!" "'E's got 'is feet on the furniture Mr. Phillips."

Sometimes Cecil or Edna had to make the interruptions themselves.

"Take your head off the wallpaper." "Leave the fish alone— you'll knock the tank over!"

But somehow or other the meetings got going, and with nothing else to keep them coming but the fact that they enjoyed it, still the kids poured in, week after week. The seating problem was eased in a mysterious way. One day, Edna got up and went downstairs to make the early morning tea. She looked out of the window and blinked. Woodenly staring back at her were two, long benches, the sort that were found in Victorian Sunday School rooms. There was no note, no one called to explain, but for months after those benches held up the bottoms of scores of children. During the week, they were kept in the garden, then every Sunday morning the house furniture was moved and the benches were carried in, dried off, cleaned up, and made ready for the weekly invasion.

To hold the attention of 50 or more estate children of mixed age range in conditions that would send a day school teacher screaming for early retirement was no small achievement, and it became clear Cecil had remarkable gifts for communicating the Bible to youngsters. But he soon realized that fun though it all was, the hour on a Sunday was not enough. Some of those Knowle West problems that had given it its notoriety were showing up right there on his living room floor. Children who were sullen or withdrawn, or who flared up suddenly, were making appeals in code for help. To understand these appeals and answer them, Cecil knew he had to get to know these children in depth. A clever artist and a modeler, he started handcraft classes for them in the week. Poor Mrs. P! Can you imagine wanting to cook and finding 50 plaster models drying in the oven?

But this relationship-building paid off, and as it developed, so the adventures became more ambitious. There was, for example, the trip to a big park about eight miles from Bristol. They went by a moving truck driven by Mr. Phillips' brother, the children hanging on to the rope ties usually used for holding beds and wardrobes from tumbling into the road. The tailgate was still down and the last of the excited bunch still scrambling onto the road when the first "E's fell in!" reached them from the boating lake. "E" was being stripped and dried when the park-keeper came rushing over, wildly pointing.

"Is that your lot over there?"

"Over there" was the middle of the lake, and yes, it was Mr. P's lot—12 of them, standing in a rowing boat designed for four. But not to worry. The boat was soon carrying its correct capacity again, the other passengers having left the quick, wet way. The handful of helpers spent most of the afternoon trying to get clothes dry, and the journey home saw "flags" flying over the tailgate, the last desperate attempt at the task.

Not to be discouraged, Cecil and Edna decided next on a camp. The three adult workers who had come to join them from a local church were horrified. They could see nothing but trouble ahead, and refused to have anything to do with it. But Cecil had seen such progress in the youngsters, with some of them becoming Christians and making spiritual growth, he believed all would be well. A friendly Christian farmer lent a field, and a local scout troop lent them tents, while a parent took all the gear down in his truck. There was no trouble, the experience became embedded on the kids' memories forever, and Cecil praised the Lord.

With the numbers still growing, it became clear that as elastic-sided as the house seemed to be, it was coming nearer and nearer to splitting at the seams. The obvious solution was to apply for the use of the Social Centre at the top of Filwood Broadway. But the caretaker put his foot down.

"I'm not having any religious group in here. I've had them before, and they always cause trouble. You won't find me opening up on a Sunday for them, and that's final!"

Without the caretaker's cooperation it was impossible, the committee explained to Cecil. Next day, a minister who had heard of the committee's decision called.

"Look here," he began, "you can't get the Social Centre for your Sunday School. My place has been empty for years. Bring your youngsters to me and let them join in with us."

Was this God's answer? Cecil didn't think so. In fact, his reaction was surprising in its vehemence: "If you've been here for so many years and your place is empty, what on earth have you been doing? There are hundreds of kids here. Your place should be full."

The minister left, slamming the door. Cecil bit his lip, wondering if he had gone too far. But the man had touched him on a raw spot. Cecil had now got so immersed in the problems and needs of the estate, he could not understand how anyone could be content to maintain a "Christian" work and not get thoroughly involved. So he was content to let the offer pass him by. The building was some distance away anyway.

It took a year's solid praying before, at last, the caretaker at the Social Centre relented. But when he did, his attitude had so been softened that he became one of the greatest friends of the work. Amazingly, on the Saturday before the Sunday School was to move into the Social Centre for the first time, the two benches fell apart in the garden.

But for all the success of the work, it was taking its toll. Cecil had had yet another spinal operation, and he was often ill. Sometimes, he would have to hold a meeting from his bed. The wear and tear on the house was terrific. Furniture wore, crockery broke, there was endless feeding of young mouths at Sunday teatimes, and always the chronic lack of money. The government "National Assistance" for unemployed and disabled people was barely adequate for any normal family, but it was never meant to cope with a thriving Sunday School. And needless to say, Cecil's young "parishioners" were hardly able to keep them going with their collection pennies. But the Lord undertook, sometimes in wonderful ways.

Once, Cecil was taken ill and had to lie on boards on the floor conducting the prayer meeting. The meeting over, Edna put on her coat to go to the shops. She checked her purse, and found nothing.

"Perhaps some money might have slipped down behind the cushions," Cecil suggested helpfully from the carpet. Everyone hunted, running their hands down the back of every chair, and along every crease and fold that coins could possibly have gotten into. Edna shrugged her shoulders.

"Well, Cec, looks like a fast day today."

Then one young girl said, "Mr. Phillips, we believe in prayer, don't we? God knows your needs—let's ask Him."

It was something Cecil could hardly say no to. They prayed. And while they were still speaking, there was a knock at the door. The girl ran to open it, and came back in less than a minute holding an envelope.

"It was a gentleman," she said. "He wouldn't give his name, just said to give this to you, Mr. Phillips."

Cecil slit the envelope with his little finger. Could it be . . . dramatic answers to prayer happened to others, not ordinary people like them . . . but, yes, there it was, in his fingers, a five-pound note.

"Before you call, I will answer, says the Lord," Cecil quoted from memory as he led his little group in profound thanksgiving.

Yet for all that it was a strain. Though the use of the Social Centre had eased the pressure on the house to some extent, there was still a constant stream of callers. There might be as many as 30 knocks on the back door (it was always the back, never the front) during the day. Children would come asking Mr. Phillips to see their dad who was dying, or talk to their mum who was threatening to leave. Adults called too who were in trouble or who were lonely. Without trying, or wanting, and without any human appointment, Cecil had become a true pastor. Not only people from the estate, but others somehow got to know about him and Edna, and came to bathe in the warmth of the relaxed Christian atmosphere of their always-open home. University students who came to lead a service found themselves coming again and again to get counsel and help from this untutored man whose grammar and spelling did such strange things with the Queen's English. And in spite of his ill health (his heart had developed problems, to combine with his almost perpetual back pain) he spent time visiting old folk, holding services for deaf girls, and getting involved with the local welfare organization.

The time had come, Cecil felt, when he would have to pull out. As much as he knew the Lord was blessing their "open home." Keith and Tricia needed quiet to do their school homework, and space to have their own friends in. In fact, the whole family needed *privacy*. It became the most desirable goal of their lives, just to have somewhere to call their own without the ceaseless tramp of feet through their sitting room and the endless knocking at the door.

After a long chat together, Cecil and Edna decided to move. They wrote out their application to the council for a house transfer, explaining the restrictions on their family life. A few days later a reply came from the council. In view of his poor health and the needs of his growing children, the council viewed his application with sympathy, and were pleased to be able to offer him another house, with two rooms downstairs instead of one, and a bus stop right outside to help him be mobile. The address was 98 Creswicke Road,—*Knowle West!*

Cecil could have cried. He stood there, the paper shaking in his hand as his fist clenched in frustration. "Knowle West! Is that the only place in Bristol they know?"

Edna was disappointed too. She had been Cecil's tireless co-worker all through the six years or so the work had been going, enduring in a single day enough to send many a lesser woman fleeing to the divorce court. As much as she shared Cecil's faith and worked wholeheartedly with him, believing it was a team effort, she too longed for peace and quiet, and freedom from the responsibility of other people's troubles.

"What are we going to do, Cec?" she asked him, making her disappointment as best she could.

"I'm going to turn it down, that's what. I'm going to tell them they've *got* to move me off the estate. Fetch me the writing pad. Let's see—it's Saturday. If I put it in the post today, they'll get it by Monday." Edna handed him the pad; he pulled a chair up to the table and took out his pen as he sat down. His pen pressed into the paper with determination. Within a few minutes the letter was lying at the bottom of the mailbox down the street waiting collection.

It was a bit of a miserable weekend. The Sunday School meeting lacked the usual zip. A cloud seemed to hang over everything. Sunday night Cecil was even more restless than usual. (Sleep was always difficult for him because of the pain.) Edna seemed uneasy as well.

Monday morning Edna had a quiet time with the Lord and found He had something to say to her. She tried to push it out of her mind, but it was not good. As she read her Bible and prayed it became quite clear to her what her Lord wanted. Quietly, without telling Cecil where she was going, she slipped on her hat and coat and went out through the door. There was no time to lose. The bus seemed to take an age covering the three miles or so into the heart of Bristol. Eventually, she was sitting in front of a desk in the council house explaining to the kind-looking man opposite.

"You see, we would really like that house you offered us after all. I'm sorry to be such a nuisance, but is it possible to disregard the letter you've had from my husband this morning?"

The man pushed his glasses up on his forehead and

squeezed his eyes with his first two fingers and thumb, his face wrinkling.

"Well, Mrs. Phillips, I'd help if I could, but I think a letter has already gone to the next in line for Creswicke Road. Still, I'll just check for you."

He reached for the phone, and pressed buttons to get an internal number. Mrs. Phillips watched anxiously as he explained things to his colleague, trying to pick up from his nods and grunts what was going on at the other end. He placed the phone down carefully and looked wonderingly at Mrs. P.

"You're extremely lucky," he said. "We never do this. Once an offer is refused, then that's it. But I understand the letter to the next applicant is still on my colleague's desk, and he is willing for you to have the house, provided you move in within two days."

Mrs. Phillips almost shouted "Hallelujah" as she flew out of the council house. The only thing was, how would she explain to Mr. P? She needn't have worried. He had had the nagging feeling at the back of his mind that to move off the estate would be to move out of the Lord's will, and Edna's confession only sealed the conviction. He dare not fight against the Lord.

Creswicke Road, if anything, proved even more demanding than Connaught Road, for now the children they had first begun with were teenagers and needed a different approach; yet still the younger children's work had to be kept going because there were ever more little ones to fill up the gaps their older brothers and sisters left. A local church sent helpers, but for many, Cecil's standards were too high. He didn't want clever people or theologically-trained people, for he knew God used the weak and foolish, but he did want committed people. "It's no use just coming for an hour on a Sunday," he would tell them. "You've got to be here in the week, getting to know them, being involved in their lives." Few were willing to accept the challenge. Often he felt alone. He could be very critical of the traditional Christian scene, seeing it as lacking reality. He still believed that true Christianity was always compassionate and always had its sleeves rolled up ready to do whatever needed to be done, whether it was to preach a sermon or to fetch an old person's coal.

He kept going to the very end. The Sunday before he died, he took Sunday School and preached in the evening service. But on the following Thursday he noted in his diary, "Found I could not walk up the Broadway—too much pain." And then, on the Sunday night, his heart finally gave out. He was 58.

His funeral was a time of rejoicing and a witness to persevering faith. As someone who knew him well said, "It was when he was weakest that he had most spiritual power; God's strength was made perfect in weakness."

Typically, he left instructions that his ashes should be put around the rose trees where they would do most good.

Edna lived on another 12 years, a "mother in Israel" to the estate of Knowle West, before she too died, succumbing to cancer.

In a way the work died with them, for although the Sunday School continues under the auspices of a local church, the heart of the work that was their open home is gone. And yet the work does still live on in the changed lives of those Cecil and Edna, God's ordinary saints, led to the Lord and influenced. I thank God I am one.

7

William and Catherine Booth

The ancient city of Nottingham, almost in the very center of England, boasts two sons famous for helping the poor. The one, Robin Hood, achieved his ends with a band of men armed with bows and knives who robbed and killed. The other, William Booth, achieved his with an army of men and women carrying Bibles and trombones for weapons, whose aim was to give life and do good, even to those who opposed them most cruelly.

If you go just a mile or two past Nottingham Castle you come to William Booth's birthplace, 12 Nottintone Place, a small, tall, upended shoebox of a house, three stories high. There, in one of the tiny upstairs rooms, William was born on April 10, 1829, to small-time builder Samuel and his wife Mary Moss Booth.

As Wiliam took his first cuddle from his mother, in the next county of Derbyshire, another baby, Catherine Mumford, born three months earlier, was taking in more and more of the world around her, conveying high intelligence with every lively look from her dark eyes and each curiosity-prompted action. Her father John was an inventive sort of man himself. A coach-builder by trade, he later made some of the first baby buggies, to the benefit of Catherine's own children.

The homes of the two infants were strikingly different in their religious atmosphere. William's parents observed the formalities. William was baptized as an infant and was forced to attend the parish church by his non-attending father. His mother observed the moral code of her day, but there was no real awareness of the gospel that her son was to preach so effectively later.

In contrast, Catherine's home was Christian in the puritan tradition. The strictness of her parents—particularly her mother—was never regretted by Catherine, who developed under her parents a strong moral sense. She grew up caring passionately about right and wrong. She treated her dolls as though they were people who had to be cared for, and her love of animals was so strong that it even found its way years later into the Salvation Army *Orders for Soldiers.*

Catherine only had a short time at school. Her more than competent mother taught her in her early years. When she did go to school, she contracted curvature of the spine. So, at 14 years old she found herself having to spend months lying on her stomach. Her incredible intelligence then really showed itself, as she educated herself with a reading program that a university student would have found difficult. She made copious notes of difficult books such as *Analogy of Religion* by Bishop Butler (John Wesley's old adversary), and huge volumes of doctrine and church history. Her voracious reading made her a firm follower of John Wesley's teachings. Yet, like

Wesley's own early years, for all her reading she lacked the assurance that she really *was* saved—that she was truly God's child.

About the time that Catherine was stricken down by her disability, William was struck by his own crisis. When William was 13 years old, his father went bankrupt and within a year Mr. Booth had died. The family's financial plight was dire. William's promising school career came to an abrupt end and he went out to earn his bread (and bread for the family) as an apprentice pawnbroker. As such, he came into contact with poverty from both sides of the counter; his own home, and the poor, destitute wretches who would bring their very clothes as pledge for a small sum to get food. William developed a huge distaste for his trade; yet paradoxically, it was for many the one thing that kept them from starvation.

By now, William had tired of the parish church, and able to choose his own place of worship, attached himself to the Methodists. There, "Wilful Will," as he often got called, heard preaching the like of which he had not heard before. One night in 1844, around 11 o'clock, walking home from a meeting, he was filled with a sudden spiritual exaltation and saw with immediate clarity he had to renounce sin, and that meant putting past misdeeds right wherever he could. One of his first acts was to tell his employer he would no longer work on a Sunday; he was instantly fired. But he was given his job back when this boss realized he had lost his best employee.

Almost from the first, Booth began to preach his new found faith; in the street, in cottages, in fact, wherever he could. And also from the first he began to see that the gospel was for the poor—and this realization got him into trouble.

One Sunday evening in Broad Street Chapel, the congregation of Methodist worthies were singing their hearty but decorous way through a hymn, when the loud metallic clunk of the heavy cast-iron latch being lifted on the outer wooden door and the gentle breeze of air as it opened announced there were latecomers. Churchgoers the world over can never resist a look around at such a time, and Broad Street was no exception. Curiosity turned to distaste, if not downright disgust at what they saw. In marched the tall, bony, raven-haired 17-year-old Booth pushing on in front of him a ragged bunch of none-too-willing worshipers who had obviously been drummed up from the alleys and backstreets of darkest Nottingham. To make his "crime" worse, William steered his flock to the plum seats of the class-conscious chapel. Afterwards, William was sternly rebuked. If tears are possible in heaven, Wesley must have wept.

Something altogether happier was happening in the Mumford home (by now in London) at this time. Catherine was still searching for the peace of God that all her piety and moral worth denied her. She had prayed and prayed, and still she was not sure. Was she, or was she not, "born again"? On the night of June 14, 1846, just before she went to sleep, she put her Bible and hymnbook under her pillow, and prayed the same words she had prayed many nights just before falling asleep.

"O God, please let me wake up knowing that you *have* accepted me. For Jesus' sake, Amen."

In the morning, she found to her unutterable joy, that her prayer was answered. Like her mentor Wesley, her heart was "strangely warmed" within her. She rushed into her mother to tell her the good news, and for months after, she experienced greater happiness than she had ever known before.

Her zeal for the Lord was immediate. She wanted to worship where she would find people who loved the Lord as she did—but found even the new Reformed Methodists lacked a vital "something." Sometimes her ill health forced her to go to the nearer Congregational chapel, and there she did hear preaching which blessed her bubbling, earnest heart. Except on one occasion.

The minister had the temerity to preach a sermon demonstrating the inferior status of women. It was fairly orthodox for the day. But the learned divine hadn't reckoned on the attractive dark haired 21-year-old, whose beauty masked a mind at least equal to his own. Through his door that week there came a wad of paper which was not so much a letter as a small booklet. Catherine developed a scriptural argument for the equality of the sexes that was pioneering for its time—and which some sections of the Christian church have not caught up with yet.

While Catherine was sorting out her differences with Dr. Thomas, William had flown the nest and had taken up residence in London. He combined pawnbroking (which he hated) with preaching (which he loved). His secular master was hard, but so was his chapel. The stewards refused to renew his church membership because of his open-air work.

However, a rich shoe-shop owner, Edward Rabbits, stepped in and offered to support him for three months if William would give up secular work for full-time evangelism. In accepting the offer, William did not realize the mighty work of God he was beginning; neither did he realize another blessing that was about to descend on him to envelop him for his lifetime. It just so happened that Edward Rabbits also knew Catherine Mumford.

It was on Good Friday, April 10, 1852, that the young couple fell in love. It was at a meeting that Rabbits invited William to attend. Later, William was asked to escort Catherine safely home and found himself alone with her for the first time.

She wrote in later years, "That little journey will never be forgotten by either of us . . . . As William expressed it, 'it seemed as if God flashed simultaneously into our hearts that affection which . . . none of the changing vicissitudes with which our lives have been so crowded has been able to efface' . . . . Before we reached my home we both felt as though we had been made for each other."[1]

At 18, Catherine had thought, "I could be most useful to God as a minister's wife." She also felt "he" should be "dark, tall, and for preference called William." Not many girls' fancies become fact with such devastating accuracy.

Next day William visited Catherine and disclosed his feelings and she hers. There were further daily meetings, and the certainty that they loved each other was never in doubt. But there was something even more important to be considered. Catherine consented to betrothal on the one condition William was absolutely certain it was God's will. William's problem stemmed from the uncertainty of his future. His arrangement with Rabbits was only a temporary one. Would God have Catherine wed a man with no home, no daily job, no money?

In addition, Mrs. Mumford became somewhat critical of William. So all in all, Catherine and William decided it would be best to be just friends.

William still lacked a positive "sign," though certain of his love. Catherine refused to take engagement as a "step in the dark." At last the "controversy" (William's word) was settled, and hand in hand he and Catherine knelt before God at Catherine's sofa, May 13, 1852, and pledged themselves to each other and to God.

They didn't marry for another three years, the intervening time being taken up with William's short training as a minister of the New Connexion of Methodists, and his first circuit of churches 100 miles from London. But the time was well spent. While William was developing his craft with great success, Catherine found God was giving her a burden for the poor every bit as great as William's. She told William in one of her love letters about "a poor, degraded, sinking drunkard, living in Russell Gardens. What I feel every time I see him I cannot describe, but I am *decided,* I will go and invite him here."[2]

Their patient courtship reached its goal at last, and they were married in London on June 16, 1855. Immediately they plunged into their work. William was preaching all over the place, his health and breakneck pace forcing an insurance company to put up his life insurance premium because they feared he would not last a year! Poor Catherine's health suffered too, and she had to be left at home quite often to endure yet more separation. They were content as long as God's will was being done. It was impossible to deny that the Lord seemed to have put a particular power into William's preaching. Sometimes the crowds could not be accommodated, even in the great barns of buildings the Victorians loved to build as their chapels.

Given a settled pastorate to look after, William was still in demand from one end of the New Connexion territory to the other. But there were ominous rumblings from people in the hierarchy of the denomination. Instead of welcoming the young evangelist as a bringer of new life, they criticized him for his "revivalist" methods. He was following Wesley closer than he knew, for like him he was to be rejected by his own church.

Before the break came, however, Catherine took a step that was of vital importance for their future work.

Pentecost Sunday morning, 1860, William was preaching in his chapel at Gateshead. Catherine was in the pew below with their young son. She was not expecting anything particular, she said, but then "I felt the Spirit come upon me . . . it seemed as if a voice said to me, 'Now, if you were to go and testify, you know I would bless it to your own soul as well as to the souls of the people.'" She tried to resist, and had a verbal battle with the devil, who told her she would look a fool. "That did it!" said Catherine. She determined she would be a fool for Christ's sake, and with rapidly-beating heart went up to the surprised William in the pulpit, who after a brief word with her told the congregation his wife wanted to say something. She told them what had happened, and William, in tune with the Spirit himself, announced his wife would preach that evening. She did—to a packed chapel. She never looked back. The

Booths were now not "evangelist and wife," but an evangelistic team. The people loved it, and loved them.

But the clouds continued to gather, as the New Connexion tried to curb William's "revivalism." After various compromises were attempted, the inevitable happened, and fully supported by Catherine (who herself had shouted "Never!" from the public gallery at one such compromise proposed at a conference), William resigned.

So after six years of marriage, and a young family to be fed, they found themselves with no church, and no income.

It was approaching midnight. Catherine, exhausted from her own preaching that night, waited up as she always did for William, who had been preaching elsewhere. Since their break with the Methodist New Connexion, things had been tough financially for them and their six children, but some campaigns in different parts of the country, and now these London opportunities had helped them through.

At last she heard the latch lift, and two or three footsteps later William was in the room facing his beloved Kate as she sat by the fire. As always, each heart leapt to the other, but this time William did not throw himself at her in a passionate kiss. He stood there for a brief moment, a strange look in his eye, and then he eased himself into the chair opposite Catherine, who was eyeing him quizzically. William's mouth moved into different shapes for a few seconds as he felt for the right words.

"Darling, I've found my destiny!" he blurted out.

Quickly then, in a torrent, he poured out how, on the way back from preaching, he had to walk through the London East End district of Whitechapel. He had gone past the pubs and the gin palaces, rowdy, noisy places, with people drunk inside, and people drunk outside, brawls and fights as common as the cobblestones. He had seen the children—ragged, barefoot, thin, neglected. There had been the houses, terrible slums, with leaky roofs, broken windows and doors. He had sensed the stagnant atmosphere of hopelessness which people seemed to accept as the natural air to breathe, as though there were no other. The only heaven was the drunkenness the cheap and plentiful liquor gave.

"Where can you go and find heathen such as these?" he went on. "Kate, we've got to do something. These people are our responsibility."

Catherine was in a turmoil. On the one hand she was thrilled with the vision. But on the other, as a practical wife and mother bringing up six children with a seventh on the way, she shuddered at the awesome burden. Preaching at church campaigns where there was a measure of assured support was a struggle, but manageable. To strike out on their own with no backing, deliberately choosing to preach to poverty-stricken people who could not support themselves, let alone an uninvited evangelist, was quite another. But if God was in it . . . . And so Catherine said, "Well, if you feel you ought to stay, we have trusted the Lord once for our support, and we can trust Him again."[3]   Her reply was more out of loyalty than enthusiasm, but it was enough for William, and enough for the Lord.

Those early days in Whitechapel with William pitching a tent on an old Quaker burial ground were not brilliantly successful, but there was one notable convert who was a kind of first-fruits. Peter Monk, an Irish prize-fighter, became a staunch ally, acting as Booth's bodyguard when the going got rough. He was particularly useful on occasions such as the time the guy-ropes were cut and the tent fell down on the crowd inside. Booth shouted to Monk, "Go outside and pull up the tent while I carry on with the preaching!"

They managed to get the use of a dance hall, and like D.L. Moody a few years earlier, spent Saturday nights cleaning the place up and carrying chairs in. All sorts of odd places, some of them smelling to high heaven from their ordinary use as fish stores or whatever, were used for meetings. But the work went on—and grew. Where the money came from—well, it came from God; but the channels he used to supply were various, from Samuel Morley, a wealthy industrialist, to the workers now attaching themselves to the Booths, willing, like their leaders, to give their very lives if only souls might be saved.

Over the next decade or so, the Booths saw the mission (now called simply the Christian Mission) grow at an amazing rate. Three years after their momentous decision in 1865 to commit themselves to the East End there were 13 "preaching stations" and 140 services were held every week. By 1877 the number was doubled, and two years later, with the work spreading at forest-fire rate, the preaching stations numbered 81.

The Booths soon gave up the idea of trying to feed their raggle-taggle converts into the established churches. The Broad Street Chapel experience of long ago was repeated too many times. For these folk, converted out of the hovels where a clergyman's foot rarely if ever trod, the Christian Mission was the only church they knew.

The couple learned some more lessons early on. The first was the power of testimony. One night, William felt he was getting nowhere with his 1,200 strong congregation. As close to the poverty-line as he was himself, nevertheless he had the wonderful security of the home and family, and somehow his unhappy, depressed hearers could not relate to him. On an impulse, he summoned to the platform an elderly gypsy hawker, a convert of recent weeks, and asked him to tell his story. Immediately, the audience was gripped.

"I shall have to burn all those sermons of mine and go in for the gypsy's,"[4] he told his son.

Another lesson was that the gospel is a practical affair. It was no good preaching to a man with an empty stomach if you didn't show the gospel was real by feeding him. So as well as the constant preaching, indoors and out, house-to-house visiting, and Bible and tract distribution, there were soup kitchens, poverty relief, penny banks to help people save, evening classes to teach reading and basic math to adults and children meetings to encourage people to give up alcohol, reading rooms, and even assistance with emigration. By 1862 there were five "Food for the Million" shops. Christmas 1868 was the last the Booth family ever saw merely as a family event. Coming home from the service he had led, William was so appalled by the degregation of the people he passed in the street, as they huddled in doorways and endured the cold, he decided that every Christmas thereafter was to be shared with the poor. He kept the pledge to the end.

Some powerful workers came alongside them. Not least was their eldest son, Bramwell. Shy, diffident, so different from his aggressive father, yet he became one of the chief mainstays of the work. Another was George Scott Railton. Having already given up a well-paid job to become a part-time Methodist missioner, he read William's pamphlet, *How to Reach the Masses with the Gospel.* "These are the people for me!" he said, packing his bags to come to London.

One of the most colorful of Booth's colleagues was to play an unwitting part in bringing about the shape of the work as we know it today.

Elijah Cadman had been a sweep-boy at six, clambering up narrow chimneys, dislodging the soot for his boss below. As a teenager, he opened a boxing saloon, and was something of a fighter himself. He was converted through watching a public hanging, when a friend had said, "That's what you'll come to one day, Elijah." It was probably meant as a joke, but it shook him to the core. He turned to God, smashed up his own boxing saloon, and became an extrovert evangelist using a great handbell to raise the crowds. It was almost inevitable that such a man should be attracted to the Christian Mission, and soon he was on Booth's team.

The year 1877 saw Cadman sent off to pioneer Whitby (the Mission had long expanded beyond the East End of London). He used every brash method he could think of, and one of his ploys was to advertise himself as Captain Cadman, because the Yorkshire fishing town was full of skippers from the boats. When Booth came up to take some meetings, Cadman thought, "If I'm 'captain,' then what's he?" William arrived to find himself billed as "General of the Hallelujah Army." He was not displeased, but certainly had no idea of adopting the title permanently.

But a few months later, the Christian Mission skin was finally sloughed off to make way for the splendid new form.

William Bramwell and Railton were with a flu-laden William in the Booth bedroom checking over the proofs of their annual report.

THE CHRISTIAN MISSION

under the superintendence
of the Reverend William Booth
is

A VOLUNTEER ARMY

Railton's reading out loud was interrupted by an indignant Bramwell. In his mind was how the part-time soldiers of Britain, the "volunteers," were laughed at for their amateurism.

"I'm not a 'volunteer,'" he cried, "I'm a regular, or nothing!"

His father caught his breath. Bramwell's words were a shaft of light cutting through his flu-befuddled brain. He strode across to Railton and snatched the pen from his hand. Excitedly, he scratched through the offending word. The eight-page report went back to the printers proudly announcing that The Christian Mission was "A SALVATION Army."

The army motif, which had been just beneath the surface for a while quickly caught on once it was out in the open. Mission halls became "citadels," prayer became "knee drill," and death became "promotion to glory." The workers took on military ranks, though it was a while before William himself was willing to take on Cadman's earlier inspired titling as permanent. But the most obvious militarizing of the Mission's structure was almost accidental.

The city of Salisbury is one of the most beautiful, sedate, and photogenic places in England. Its crowning glory is a cathedral with a soaring, elegant spire, immortalized in painting by none less than Constable. In such a place as this, the new Army with its street meetings and revivalist preaching was not welcome. In fact a committee was formed of citizens exasperated by "the noise and nuisance caused and created by the proceedings of the Salvation Army." The little band of workers felt very vulnerable. It so happened that a local builder named Charles Fry and his three sons were also brass-bandsmen. When the Fry's offered to act as a bodyguard, they also decided to bring along their instruments to accompany the open air meetings. From little acorns, oaks grow; and from that impromptu quartet grew the music ministry of the Salvation Army that has played in almost every country on earth to a total audience of millions.

Mention of the opposition at Salisbury brings us to an aspect of the early Army that can only make us marvel at their resolve. The hostility they faced was enormous. Some were sent to prison, "guilty" of various technical offences to do with disturbing the peace; others suffered personal injury from mobs, which were often organized with the cooperation of the local authorities. There was one group, calling themselves the Skeleton Army, dedicated to silencing the Salvationists through fearful intimidation. Often, those on the receiving end were just young girls, many from sheltered backgrounds, won by the challenge of adventurous, bold Christianity. For such girls to be under siege in their "citadel" (which in reality might be a ramshackle building, little better than a shed) must have been frightening indeed. Added to that, many of these early workers were not strong because of the sparse diet they lived on. Money was as tight as could be.

But in spite of everything, the work prospered, and gradually respect was won, sometimes from unexpected quarters. God used the Army to open England's eyes to the terrible poverty and evil being nursed in the bosom of the world's richest, most powerful nation. With the help of a remarkable journalist, W.T. Steadman, the villianous "white-slave" traffic in young girls was exposed (which noble work cost Steadman a prison sentence, Bramwell escaping the same fate by the skin of his teeth). Then Steadman helped Booth write one of the most influential social documents in Britain's history: *In Darkest England and the Way Out,* a devastating analysis of the ills of the time, with daring and imaginative remedies. It was a project William had ordered when having driven across London Bridge one dark night in a cab, he saw scores "sleeping rough." "Bramwell, do something!" he commanded in his imperious manner.

But at about the same time as *Darkest England* was published, darkness of a different sort was stalking the Booths.

At the beginning of 1888, Catherine confided to Bramwell she had found a small lump in her breast. Her alarmed son immediately insisted she should see a doctor. The doctor's diagnosis and prognosis were grim: cancer, and immediate surgery was her only hope to avert death within two years. She bore the news bravely. William was shattered. Other medical opinions were sought, but all said the same. Desperately, "cures" were tried; eventually, Catherine consented to the surgery, in those days, primitive and painful. But the cancer rampaged on.

The Booths rented a small house on the east coast, not too far from London, so that Catherine could rest as much as possible, and William could come and see her with reasonable ease. He did most of his work on *Darkest England* there, interrupting his scribbling willingly to see to her every need. He found it almost unbearable to witness the awful pain she was going through, aghast at the hemorrhaging that soaked the sheets in blood. It was the first time in his life as a Christian that he found even the foundations of his faith rocked as he cried inwardly, "Why, God, why?"

But Catherine, mother of the Salvation Army, was not letting go. Her philosophy was summed up in something she put in a letter: "Don't be concerned about your dying. Only go on living well, and the dying will be alright."[5]

On Thursday, October 2, 1890, it looked as though she was going. Catherine and William spent the night together alone, everyone else sent out from the room. Pain and tenderness intertwined in a night of reaffirmed love. But she survived that night, and the next. Then on the Saturday afternoon, after each of the children kissed her tenderly, the end came. William embraced her. "Pa!" she whispered, and she was gone.

Following the funeral service and procession, when 3,000 Salvationists lined the streets, the general standing upright in his carriage, William knew he had to go on working. Half of him was gone, but there must be no let-up. A great battle was about to break over his head with the publication of *In Darkest England*. No one likes having his sins and faults revealed, least of all a state with a proud history such as Britain. The epic publication was challenged on every front. But Booth and his fellow Salvationists fought on, and led the way by instituting many of the reforms themselves. They set up model factories, established farm colonies, gave people a new start overseas, and began a labor exchange. Gradually, the authorities came to accept the need for change, and the social welfare of the United Kingdom today, imperfect though it is, owes not a little to the magnificent pioneering work of the "Blood and Fire" Army.

For another 22 years William toiled on. He traveled thousands of miles by sea and land. He undertook arduous motor tours to preach, becoming one of the sights of Britain as he arrived in towns and villages, in a cloud of exhaust smoke, white beard flowing, then standing up to let fly his mighty verbal volleys. In those years he became the guest of royalty and cabinet ministers. From being the "off-scouring of the world," he had become almost a national institution. But he never let this fame turn his head or divert him from his vision. Near the very end of his life, his sight almost gone, he delivered a passionate declaration at the Albert Hall, London.

"While women weep as they do now, I'll fight; while little children go hungry as they do now, I'll fight; while men go to prison as they do now, in and out, in and out, I'll fight; while there yet remains one dark soul without the light of God, I'll fight—I'll fight to the very end."[6]

For William, the end was not very far off. An operation to try to save his remaining sight was unsuccessful. He lay ill, still chiding Bramwell to do something for the homeless. Then on Tuesday, August 20, 1912, after two days' unconsciousness, his breath finally ceased. The announcement was posted next morning in the window of the Army's headquarters:

"The General Has Laid Down His Sword."

Once, Bramwell asked his father the secret of his strength. William told him it stemmed back to long ago when he had knelt in Broad Street Chapel, Nottingham, and told God that He should have all that there was of William Booth.

Booth's daughter Eva heard about her brother's question and her father's answer.

"No," she said, "that wasn't really his secret. His secret was that he never took it back."

For further reading: *The General Next to God,* by Richard Collier (Collins, London)

Catherine Booth, by Catherine Bramwell Booth (Hodder & Stoughton, London)

Notes
1. Catherine Bramwell Booth, *Catherine Booth* (London: Hodder and Stoughton, 1970), p. 63.
2. Booth, *Catherine Booth,* p. 111.
3. Booth, *Catherine Booth,* p. 228.
4. Richard Collier, *The General Next to God* (London: Collins Fontana, 1968), p. 48.
5. Collier, *The General Next to God,* p. 168.
6. Collier, *The General Next to God,* p. 220.

8

John Newton

Sometimes congregations get to feel their minister is "past it." As they've sat under their former Golden Boy, now become a White Old Man rambling in confused meanderings, they've groaned for someone to tell him to call it a day. The congregation at Saint Mary Woolnoth in London in the early 1800s believed that time had come for their venerable 80-year-old rector, Reverend John Newton. Well-loved as he was, revered by some so much that it fell just short of worship, his increasing deafness and blindness and his embarrassing knack of forgetting what he was saying made it seem as much for his own sake as for his hearers that someone should tactfully put the suggestion to him. The brave man to whom this task fell was Richard Cecil. Persevering until he had penetrated through the old man's deafness he made himself understood. Newton looked appalled and disbelieving. He filled his lungs, then let out a lion's roar.

"What! Shall the old African blasphemer stop while he can speak?"

Behind the emotional declaration lay quite a history, one of the great true adventure stories of all time.

Sea life has always been hard for the families sailors leave behind, but it was much more so in the days when ships were powered by sail. The absences would be longer, the return dates, dependent on weather, hopelessly approximate, and, there was the ever likely possibility that there would be no return at all. But young John Newton was quite glad to have his father, Captain Newton, away, for that meant he had his mother all to himself. She taught him reading, writing, and arithmetic, and shared her warm love of God with him. She impressed Bible verses on his mind, and took him with her to chapel. His father, on the other hand, was strict and showed little outward affection. But at the age of six, John's little secure maternally-centered world suddenly collapsed. His mother died of tuberculosis. In no time at all, a new stepmother was on the scene who cared not at all for him, and a boarding school with a tyrannical headmaster who wielded his cane ferociously was no improvement.

At 11 years old John's school career ended abruptly, and he found himself sailing the world with his father, interspersed with spells in his stepmother's home, generally running wild with the local kids. The early piety his mother had tried to instill seeped away in escapades and roguish pranks. A couple of brushes with death sobered him up in these impressionable years, but on the whole, he went from bad to worse. Just to drive him further the wrong way, when he was

17, a book fell into his hands which, as far as he could understand it, encouraged him to look on all his childhood upbringing as reins to be thrown off so he could run free as a wild stallion. The way to live was to work out his own philosophy and, if his heart told him to do something, then it was right, so he should do it. God existed, but not to interfere with his life. To John, it was a fascinating way of looking at things, and very enticing.

But for now he must get on with trying to earn a living. His father retired from the sea, but decided John should climb the gangplank instead of him—though his son's first attempt wasn't very encouraging. He came back from a voyage as third mate, with the captain reporting to his father, "Your son will never make a sailor!" Newton Senior thought perhaps a sea career was best avoided, so through a friend of his, Joseph Manesty, merchant in the thoroughly respectable trade of slaving, he got John a job in Jamaica as a slave overseer. It appealed to the young Newton, and he was quite excited at the thought of making his fortune in the balmy paradise of the West Indies.

A few days before he was due to sail, he had a surprise letter from an old friend of his mother's inviting him to stay for a few days. "Fine!" said Captain Newton. "I have some business I want you to do for me down that way anyway. So go ahead. But make sure you're back for your ship, mind you."

And so John fully intended to do. But when he got to the Kent house, and 14-year-old Mary "Polly" Catlett opened the door, something happened with total unexpectedness. He fell plumb in love. Cupid's arrow pierced his heart up to the feathers, and it never came out again to his dying day.

Of course, he couldn't show his feelings. Not at this stage.

Mr. and Mrs. Catlett gave him a right royal welcome, and utterly spoiled him. They made him one of the family, and insisted he call them "Aunt" and "Uncle." He had not experienced such open affection since his mother died. The upshot was he stayed three weeks instead of three days. His father was frantic, assuming the worst—perhaps an accident, or a highwayman—and when John eventually returned, having missed his boat to Jamaica, although as angry as an old sea captain can be, he forgave his son. But he felt John should learn his lesson. His punishment was that his wayward son should make a voyage as a common sailor. All John's previous trips to sea had been in officers' quarters.

If Captain Newton's intention was to drum the irresponsibility out of the young man, the project failed. But it did succeed in tearing away the last shreds of youthful innocence. John came back from an unshielded exposure to the bawdiness, crudeness, roughness, and downright vice that formed the life of the man at sea in the eighteenth century.

But his father was satisfied, and so once more used his influence to get him an officer's berth. Too trusting of his son, he unwisely allowed John to visit Polly again a few days before he was due to sail; and once more his incorrigible John was beguiled by the lovely (to him) young girl, overstayed, missed his berth, and had to face his father's wrath. Furious, Captain Newton all but finished forever with the irresponsible youth. But a much softer man in reality than John had ever perceived him, he relented, and though it must have cost his pride, procured yet one more place for him on a ship. Yet again, the plan was to be thwarted, and yet again a visit to Polly was the trigger of events. But this time John was victim, not offender.

John walked down toward the Thames River bank where he could catch the ferry across to the Kentish coast and then make the ride to his beloved Polly's house. He walked briskly with the sailor's rolling gait that even at the young age of 18 he had acquired from his time aboard ship. A group of men in the shadows, clubs and batons in hand, noted it and drew their own conclusions. Stealthily they padded towards him, then suddenly charged, pinning his arms, giving him no chance to hit out or to run away. The shock of the surprise attack passed over him, and as he saw his assailants' dress he knew in an instant why he had been set upon. It was a press gang!

The press gang was a simple, brutal, unjust but lawful way of recruiting for the Royal Navy. Volunteers were few, and the only way His Majesty's ships could be manned was to kidnap off the streets anyone who looked suitable.

John realized physical resistance was out of the question. He tried to argue his way out.

"Let me go at once!" he shouted with as much authority as he could muster. "I am a serving officer. You have no right to impress me. It is unlawful! Let me go, I command you, or you will be in trouble!"

"Shut your mouth!" one of the men sneered back. "We've heard it all before. You don't think we'd believe that yarn, do you? And if we did, d'ye think it'd make any difference?" and with choice oaths hustled him along to an inn, where he was bundled into a back room.

"Let me have one concession, I pray you," John pleaded. "Let me write a note to my father."

"He won't be able to get you out, you know that? All right—we'll get the pot boy to give you pen and ink, and you can pay him yourself to take it."

He scribbled a desperate note and urged the lad to make as much haste as he could, then settled down in dejection to await the next moves. Over the next hours, one by one other young men, frightened and cursing, were bundled into the room with him. And then at last he heard the unmistakeable voice of his father. When eventually his father was allowed into the room, his expression told the tale that he had failed to change the mind of the lieutenant in charge of the press gang. John was too good a catch, and the immediate threat of war made the strengthening of the navy too urgent.

A little later and the reluctant Navy recruit found himself in the miserable dark of below decks in HMS *Harwich,* a 50-gun man-o'-war.

He discovered his captain was named Carteret, and when he was interviewed by him had one crumb of comfort in that he was enrolled as Able Seaman rather than Ordinary Seaman.

Rough as his life on the merchant ships had been, John found Royal Navy life rougher. The very fact the crew was almost totally pressganged guaranteed it. The cat-o'-nine-tails (a savage whip) and the cane were the chief means of discipline. Still, things didn't go too badly at first. Old Captain Newton pulled strings, and John found himself promoted to midshipman, which improved his lot considerably. But his distance from God grew greater. Apart from the coarsening influence of the company, he made a friend of the captain's clerk, who subtly drew John further into the insidiuous sucking mire of the philosophy behind the book he had read years ago. Although John had some qualms about it, he became an openly avowed atheist as far as belief was concerned, and an advocate of absolute license to do what he wanted or felt like in ethics. In fact, he became something of an evangelist of atheism, successfully corrupting another shipmate, Job Lewis.

Such an arrogant attitude on top of the untamed irresponsibility he had already displayed was bound to get him into trouble. Given shore leave, he outstayed his time at Polly's more than once. Remarkably, Captain Carteret let him off with no more than a roasting from his tongue. But John was about to try the suffering Navy man's patience an oar too far.

The squadron of ships set out on a long tour of duty, but were still off the Cornish and Devon coasts when they got into enormous difficulties and had to take shelter in Torbay for repairs. Refused leave to see his father, whom he knew was in the area, John decided he would go anyway. His hope was his father could get him out of the navy. Put in charge of a shopping trip ashore, John took his chance. With the long-boat tied up at the dock and the men busy about the loading, he slipped away. His freedom was brief. One night sleeping outdoors, a few hours tramping the Devon countryside the next day, and then before he realized it he ran slap into a search party of marines. As the curious onlookers watched him marched, dishonored, back to the long-boat, John hardly dared think what might happen. He could even be hanged for desertion.

Back on board he faced his captain, whose repeated kindness and trust he had betrayed. Not that John was feeling any remorse—just fear, resentment, and a mounting bitterness. He had no God to turn to, so waited for the verdict in as manly a way as he could, to take it come what may. Carteret pronounced his verdict. John was to be flogged and to be degraded to Ordinary Seaman.

The ship's company was assembled on deck to watch what was not an unusual sight; not that the commoness made it any easier for the sufferer. John's shirt was pulled roughly off his back, and he was tied to a frame. A bosun's mate held the cat-o'-nine-tails, relishing his task. Newton was not liked on board because of his boorish manner. The mate's brawny muscles in his brown arm tensed, accumulating power; the drum rolled, and the pent-up force was unleashed, leaving with each stroke nine searing red-hot, red-running wounds.

At last, his crimson, lacerated back throbbing cruelly, that part of the ordeal was over. But the second part was only just beginning. Reduced to the lowest rank, John lost all his privileges and found himself the lowest of the low. Those he had ordered about were now ordering him. He was facing five years of absolute hell. If there was a way out he would make sure he found it.

His chance came as the ship lay anchored off the Guinea

coast of Africa in May 1745. He happened to have the good fortune (in later life he believed it was God's providence) to be around as he heard that Captain Carteret was required to give two men in exchange for two who had been impressed from a slaving ship anchored nearby. Immediately Newton volunteered to be one of them, and probably because he was glad to be rid of him, Carteret agreed.

It turned out that the captain of the slaver knew John's father, so showed exceptional kindness, to which John was not very responsive. He saw it as a great liberation and wanted to exercise his philosophy of freedom to do what he liked as fully as he could. The evil conditions of the slaves on board did not touch him at all. Worse, the awful and bestial things that were done to them he became part of. Any female slave was considered fair game by the crew, and John, for all his undying love for Polly back home, indulged his animal lusts to the full.

The captain died on the voyage, and John, sensing that the mate who took over would make life difficult for him, spoke to the owner, named Clow, who was on board, asking if he could work for him. The man seemed quite taken with the idea, so shortly John found himself on land being taken to the man's home, where Clow's black woman (they were not married) held court. She was regarded as a Princess and lived like one. Her name came oddly into English as P.I. With Clow away, P.I. treated Newton abominably, especially when he was sick. He was made to live in squalor with virtually nothing to eat. When Clow returned, things improved for a while. Clow made Newton a partner in a new venture, but suddenly John was plunged into even worse degradation than he had known on the *Harwich*. Through the false report of another jealous trader, Newton had vague accusations made against him, and Clow's benevolent attitude changed instantaneously. There, in the African tropics, the law was what any man made it. Clow had his own way for dealing with Newton whom he now considered a cur. Because this sudden change happened during a period of going up and down the river collecting slaves, Newton was first chained to the deck of the small river craft. For two months he was like that with virtually no food, and subject to the tropical storms without any cover, and with no one allowed even to speak to him. Then, back at his house, Newton was fastened in slave chains and became a slave of the slaves, living an abysmal life doing menial work with the very minimum of food. P.I. greatly enjoyed seeing John's sufferings. The only way he could keep himself sane was to teach himself the geometric theorems of Euclid, drawing out the proofs in the sand with a stick.

His position was hopeless, and it seemed he must die. He took one slim chance to get help. One day, when his task involved meeting a ship with its goods used as barter for slaves, he pressed a letter to his father into a sailor's hand.

"Please, please do all you can to get it delivered!" he implored. It seemed a long shot indeed. But there was nothing else to do. For him, prayer was impossible.

But though Newton had given up on God, God had not given up on him, and a chain of events unfolded to get him out of his dreadful mess.

The first chink of light to shine on his darkness was the offer of another trader to Clow to take Newton on, and Clow agreed. Now his chains could come off; now he could live in proper accommodation and have good food. He would be able to wear shoes on his feet, and there would be no slaves telling him what to do; best of all there would be no P.I., with her incessant mockery.

In fact, things worked out beyond his wildest dreams. Transferred to help manage a new factory, he and his partner saw prosperity increase. Newton began to thoroughly enjoy life in this beautiful untamed continent, where anyone who would could carve out his own kingdom. It took physical strength, it took courage—and a willingness to sink any moral scruples. But the material rewards were great.

Then came one of those remarkable coincidences that later John saw as the unmistakable hand of God. He and his partner where short of items for barter in order to complete a purchase of slaves from the black slave traders. If only a ship would sail in. They expected none, but they decided to go down the coast for a look. Right on cue came a vessel, and they quickly built a fire to send a smoke signal to get the ship to anchor, which it did. Of all the ships in the world at that moment, it happened to be one of Mr. Joseph Manesty's, the friend of Captain Newton. And one of the first questions the ship's master asked was, "Do you know where I can find a Mr. John Newton?" for John's father had received his mournful letter written from the pit of despair of Clow's bondage, and had asked Manesty to help. For miracles of one man finding another, it equals if not exceed Morton's discovery of David Livingstone.

But circumstances had changed a lot since that letter of bitter hopelessness. John felt he had found his niche in life and the African life was the life for him. The Captain of the *Greyhound* was thrilled at his success at finding Newton, however, and wanted to take his prize home. He plied John with all sorts of reasons for returning. But John would have none of it until one came into his mind that the Captain would never have thought of in a million years. Polly. Was there any chance, he wondered, that he could still win her, in spite of the disgrace, and his checkered career? One thing was certain—he would never have her for his wife if he stayed. His mind was made up! He would return.

The trip back was to be nonstop. That was the good news. The bad news was that the way the trade winds blew meant that it was going to be a circuitous route westward, then north eastward, of 7000 miles. So as the 22-year-old adventurer set sail as the captain's guest, he occupied himself with his Euclid and looked for other books to pass the time. He discovered a version of the famous Christian classic by Thomas à Kempis, *The Imitation of Christ*, and read it simply as a book, not from any sense of spiritual need. In fact his life on board up to that time had been as uncooperative and boorish as ever. He delighted in swearing. Newton's speech was so offensive that the captain, who was fairly used to strong language, was moved to warn him. Newton took fiendish delight in devising new swear words.

It was the weather that changed all that. Two months into the voyage a westerly gale blew up. It raged on and on. Eight days later, he found himself reading a passage from à Kempis that brought home the uncertainty of life, and the fact that one day we have to give account of our lives. Into his atheistic mind John found the question being forced that would not be kept out: *What if these things be true?*

His unwelcome contemplation didn't prevent him going to sleep however. But later that night he was suddenly smashed awake by the fury of the storm sending the timbers of the ship into impossible contortions. He hastened out of his bunk as he saw water pouring in. Urgent shouts cut through the gale: "The ship is sinking!"

He was about to climb the ladder up to the deck when the captain shouted to him to bring a knife. He went to fetch it and a seaman climbed up to the deck ahead of him. Suddenly a huge snatching arm of a wave whisked the man overboard as though he were a peg doll. Newton stood aghast at the bottom of the ladder with the knife. If he had not been delayed by the captain's request it would have been him pitched in the boiling sea rather than the other poor seaman. But here was no place to enter into meditation. Every second was counting, as the ship pitched and rolled, and water continued to pour in. Exactly where the ship was torn was impossible to tell in the dark. The important thing was to man the pumps and baling buckets.

John took his turn, and whatever unwillingness he had

shown to join in and play his part before on the voyage was washed away in the first flood of water that woke him. He worked his end of the pump with dogged determination. It seemed impossible that the water they were getting out could ever be more than was continually coming in. Surely the ship must sink. They had to keep going. The rhythmic up-down-up of the pump seemed to part a way in the turmoil of his mind for a parade of thoughts to march through. He reflected on his life, and still that question was in his mind raised by à Kempis: *What if these things be true?*

His own experience of seamanship made him think of a way that would help the ship through, so he made his suggestion to the captain during a break from pumping. The captain was gracious enough to accept his idea, and then to his own surprise, John found himself saying, "If this will not do, the Lord have mercy upon us."

What was that? Atheist John mentioning the Lord as though He existed? He shook his head in wonder.

Day dawned and the storm was a lot less than it had been, but the seas were still rough, the waves huge, and the ship was still sinking. The whole of that day was spent in the desperate business of trying to get the ship free of water. While he was working to the point of utter exhaustion at the task, John was also trying to get his mind free of the water of atheism. He began to pray after a fashion, and he wondered if he could suspend his unbelief in the Scriptures enough to assume they were true.

By evening it seemed at last they had the ship safe from sinking from the weight of the water it had taken on, but the danger was by no means over. The wind was still strong, and the creaky, leaky vessel with its torn sails was difficult to steer into the waves. If a wave came broadside, it would capsize for sure; and there was the constant threat that its timbers would shatter and the vessel break up.

They battled on, and then discovered that most of their

food had been washed overboard. Strict rationing was imposed. Meanwhile, John was still battling spiritually. He had now found a New Testament and began to study it when he could get any time. He took the Scriptures on trust, though he was still not sure if they were all true. One immediate result was that he stopped swearing, and never again took an oath on his lips.

The fifth day of the storm brought an excited shout from the lookout: "Land Ahoy!" The rising red sun showed a crimson outline on the horizon that they took to be the Irish coast. A celebration drink of the last of the brandy was ordered, but while it was still in their mouths it turned bitter as those straining their eyes to the horizon saw the "coastline" disappear in the increasing daylight. It was the seaman's equivalent of a desert mirage. There was nothing before them but open sea. Their disappointment was crushing. Despair began to threaten their morale. Things became even worse, for now they were stranded in the middle of the ocean for lack of winds. When the wind began to blow it was from the east instead of the west. Their tattered sails could make nothing of it, and they were hopelessly driven the wrong way.

Men's minds began to think strange thoughts. The captain, who had been so friendly and enthusiastic in Africa, began to look ominously at John and mutter "Jonah!" The story from the Old Testament of the prophet who disobeyed God by going on a ship, and had to be thrown overboard to save it from shipwreck, was well known to him. Could it be . . . John wondered if his end was near, not from a storm, but from a desperate captain who feared God's judgment.

It took 14 days for the contrary wind to drop, and then, at last, there was a favorable westerly. To their utter joy and delight, on the twenty-seventh day after the beginning of the disaster, their lookout spied real, solid land. The next day their crippled ship was safe in a friendly, smiling Irish harbor.

John had no doubt that he had been saved by God. He

couldn't understand much about it yet, but already he was filled with a sense of amazement that after all he had done against his Creator, he had been brought back just like the prodigal son in Jesus' parable. As he rested and recuperated, he realized there were some things he had to do to make good the change in his life.

First and foremost, he must make a proper dedication of himself to God. He went to the church at Londonderry, and there took communion. Next, he must write to his father and ask his forgiveness for the wrongs he had done him. His father replied with great joy. (Unfortunately, the two were never to meet again, for Captain Newton was on his way to Hudson's Bay to a new appointment, and would die before his three-year term was complete.) Next, he must go to Liverpool to thank Mr. Manesty for all he had done.

He duly arrived there, and to his surprise, his father's friend so took to him that he straight away offered him command of one of his slave ships, the *Brownlow*. John declined, not because as a Christian he was opposed to the slave trade— that came much later—but because humility had at last been born in him, and he realized he needed to learn before he could lead. He therefore agreed to go as mate.

So with amends made, and a new career in front, one thing remained unsettled, and it bothered him. He had hoped to hear from Polly, but no letter was waiting for him. He now had both his father's and the Catlett's consent to ask Polly to marry him, but why no word from Polly? Perhaps she did not care for him? But at last he heard from Polly's aunt that he may come down and court his sweetheart. He needed no second bidding. However, his opportunity for courtship was severely limited by the fact that he had to get back for the sailing of the *Brownlow*. The new John Newton was not going to overstay his leave!

Sad to say, however, his return to the sea seemed to make the new John Newton fade away. He neglected prayer and the

Bible, and many of his old habits reasserted themselves. Though he was so passionately in love with Polly, once back in Africa and the slaves were taken on board he did as he had done before and despicably raped one of them. God had a great deal more to do in John Newton yet; and He had His own way of doing it. John was struck down with a dreadful fever; once more he felt the closeness of death. He realized at once it was a rebuke, and turned back to the Lord, never to backslide in that way again.

With the cheap barter goods exchanged for slaves, the *Brownlow* sailed across to America, where the unfortunate cargo was exchanged for rum and tobacco, and then it was back to Liverpool to complete the shameful triangle of trade. But as yet virtually few Christians queried its rightness.

Once home, he was now offered his own command. But more important to him was the pursuit of his heart's desire in the south of England. It was now or never to propose.

He made a complete hash of the proposal; Polly refused him—twice! But Polly's own family encouraged him not to give up, and at last she accepted. His joy knew no bounds, and on February 1, 1750 they were married.

He would dearly have loved any other job but the sea at this point. To be married and then leave within months was cruel. But there was no other income, so in June he sailed away on his first slaver as Captain John Newton. It seems odd to us that he saw his Christian duty as combining holding services for the crew on Sundays with keeping rebellious slaves in order by means of thumbscrews. But the light of God dawns slowly in most people, and we are all children of our time. There are no doubt social evils to which we are blind but which our descendants will clearly see.

The end to John's slaving career and his emergence as a powerful Christian witness was not far off though. In October 1753 he went on his last trip. There were two important things that changed his course and made him seek a call from God more determinedly than ever before. One of those things was negative—a tragedy. The other was positive—a discovery.

When he began his voyage, he took on board Job Lewis, whom he had helped turn into an atheist years before. Job had become such an ardent free thinker that Newton was appalled. He worked hard to convert his old shipmate, but it was no use. The attempts proved utterly futile, and poor Job died at sea, convicted of his sin but unconverted, and with no faith in a Saviour. This depressing experience made Newton pray all the more earnestly that he might know his faith better, to help other people, and that he might be able to give up this distasteful trade, for though he did not as yet see the actual evil of slave-trading itself, to be involved with chains and shackles seemed to him no job for a Christian man.

His first prayer was answered swiftly. When he arrived at the West Indies, he came across a Captain Clunie, whom he discovered was a Christian. Clunie became to Newton what Priscilla and Aquila became to Apollos: he explained the way of God more fully. For the first time, John began to see how things all fit together in the Christian gospel. It led Newton to make a fresh surrender of his life to the God whose amazing grace had saved a wretch like him. They spent hours together, and John found his faith grew wings.

John sailed back to Liverpool with a much lighter heart than he had sailed out with. But it seemed his second prayer for some other calling was not going to be answered, for waiting for him was yet another ship which he was to command. It was still being built, but, said Mr. Manesty, when it was, it should be his to name and to sail.

But the Lord had other plans. Just before the sailing date John collapsed with a mystery illness. The new ship sailed without him, and by the time he recovered, it was far away to the south.

Then all sorts of things began to happen. He was given a job as tide surveyor in Liverpool; he met the famous evangelist, George Whitefield; and he began to give his testimony in various churches in Yorkshire. These were the immediate things that preceded the life of Christian service that goes beyond the scope of this account.

The future God had in store for "the old African blasphemer" took him into the ministry of the Church of England; there, his preaching and writing (his enormous number of letters still counsel today) blessed countless people, and, being completely non-sectarian, Christians of all denominations were his friends. He became one of the most ardent opponents of the slave trade, giving invaluable ammunition to the man who brought about its end in Britain, William Wilberforce.

But, of course, it's the writing of those superb hymns that makes John Newton still so much part of today's church, 200 years after his time.

> Amazing Grace! How sweet the sound,
> That saved a wretch like me;
> I once was lost, but now am found,
> Was blind, but now I see.

Though at the end his natural powers failed, his faith and conviction never did. His dying words summed it up: "My memory is nearly gone. But I remember two things; that I am a great sinner, and that Christ is a great Saviour."

For further reading: *Amazing Grace* by J.C. Pollock (Hodder & Stoughton, London)

9

Eric Liddell

L ittle Jenny Liddell, upset and near to tears, came running in to her mother. Mrs. Liddell immediately put down her sewing and enfolded her daughter close, her gentle hand smoothing back her hair, comforting and consoling.

"Now, Jenny, what's the matter? Why are you crying?"

"It's Eric, Mama—he is going to get better, isn't he?"

Mrs. Liddell looked out anxiously through the open window of the Siaochang mission house to see her son, one year older than Jenny, stumbling and picking himself up."

"Och, my sweet, I'm sure he will. He's had a very bad fever, and it's gone on for a long time, but we're all praying, and I believe he'll get stronger in a wee while."

Jenny, though she had learned to trust everything her mother said—it was that kind of family—was still not sure.

"But . . . but . . . he keeps wobbling . . . and Mrs. Smith said. I heard her say it."

"Said what, darling?"

Jenny's eyes filled up again. "She said, 'That boy will never be able to run again.'"

Mrs. Liddell smiled. "We'll have to prove her wrong, won't we?"

A little while later, the Reverend James Dunlop Liddell sat with his wife and three children (the elder brother was Robert) in the carriage of the "Flying Scotsman" as it raced its noble way up the east coast of England to his beloved homeland. It was a job to tell who was more excited, he or his three children, now aged seven, five, and four, as the father pointed first to this and then to that, most of which the children looked at blankly, unable to take in much because of the speed of the train. All they had ever known as children was the Great Plain of China; the sights and sounds of oriental life were for them the "real" world. Britain, with its ever-changing pattern of town, village, and green countryside, was the foreign place. But it was to be their home for the foreseeable future. When Mr. and Mrs. Liddell returned from this, their first missionary furlough, the children would be left behind for school.

So although those precious days in father's Edinburgh were happy, they were overshadowed by the feeling that one day soon, Mama and Dad would not be there, but far, far away in China. But in those days of slow ships and no worldwide telephone, that was the accepted price of missionary service.

The next year, then, saw eight-year-old Rob and nearly-seven-year-old Eric entering the School for Sons of Missionaries. Eric was still rather weedy, but the headmaster's almost obsessional belief in the value of sports to build a boy up meant that Eric was soon developing a physique that could cope with three or four bruising rugby matches a week. (Rugby is a contact game somewhat similar to American football, but without the armor). In fact rugby became Eric's passion, with athletics in general close to it.

Not only was Eric's body strengthened at school, but also his faith. He did not have a dramatic conversion experience. It seems he never could put a finger on the exact moment when he first put his trust in Jesus Christ as his Saviour. He simply *knew* Christ, and *knew that he knew.* He had no illusions that he could make himself a Christian: it was the Holy Spirit alone who could do that. Yet he also knew that he must make a real commitment to follow Christ. Years later, in China, he would write a manual of Christian discipleship, in which he would say:

> "*Surrender is not the new birth.* The new birth should be simultaneous with, or closely following, the act of surrender, but is not identical with it. The new birth is the great work God does in us in renewing our natures. Surrender is our part."[1]

Without making a great show of his Christian faith, Eric made quiet and steady growth. He joined the Bible class (which was voluntary) and in time he became a communicant member of the Church of Scotland. He was a founder member of a Crusader's Christian Union. It may have been at this time that the keeping of his early morning quiet time first became his unbreakable habit. Certainly at school he appeared to have discovered that beautiful balance between development of the body and enrichment of the spirit that was the hallmark of his later life.

Both Liddell boys turned out to be remarkable athletes who tended to monopolize the first and second places in their school sports.

But to be front-runner at a small school of missionaries' sons is one thing; to go to the university where the cream of the national young talent surfaced was quite another. Eric did not make a big thing of his prowess; it probably never occurred to him that he had anything special in that company. But persuaded to enter the university athletics sports with very little training, and with his legs stiff from a cycle tour in the Highlands, he surprised everyone, including the favorite, by winning the 100 yards and only just being edged out in the 220 (the only race he ever lost in Scotland).

His performance meant an almost automatic selection for the university team, and soon he was winning races wherever he went—and with style. At the 1923 Inter-Universities Sport three records came crashing down as he broke the tape time after time.

Away in China, James Liddell looked forward to the news that came by the painfully slow mail. Eric's letters would be no doubt so modest that his parents would never guess he was doing anything more extraordinary than running for the bus each morning. (Though even that was not quite the same when Eric was around. Out for a training run once with some friends, a cheeky bus driver blew his horn at them, and Eric's response was to race it to the top of the hill—and win!)

The letters from Jenny would tell a different story, glowing in sisterly pride. "Every week he brings home prizes. We've nowhere to put them all." And Mr. Liddell, no mean athlete himself in his time, would smile a satisfied smile, while Mrs. Liddell would think about those fever-weakened legs. Never run again, indeed!

There was no family clash over Eric's running. The film *Chariots of Fire* invented the tension for dramatic impact. The only clash was in Eric himself over his two great sporting loves. For all the while that he was cluttering up Jenny's house with clocks and watches and rose bowls for his running, he was also piling up the points on the rugby field. He made the

university team with ease, and then came his first international cap. Another friend from the missionaries' sons' school
partnered him in vintage years for Scottish rugby. Normally
underdogs in the Five Nations Championship, in the two seasons Eric played, he was only on the losing side once. But
with the Olympics looming ahead, to say nothing of the small
matter of getting his degree, Eric decided he should concen-
trate on running, and so one of the most promising of rugby
careers was brought to a premature stop, much to the dismay
of the Scottish fans.

At this time a man entered on the scene who was to have a
decisive effect on Eric. His name was D.P. Thomson.

I myself met D.P. Thomson some years ago when he was
quite old, but still full of fire for the Lord. We sat down for a
meal together, and I happened to mention South Africa. He
chuckled and said, "It's a good job I'm not in South Africa. I
would have to say something about *apartheid* (legalized dis-
crimination aimed at non-whites). I couldn't keep quiet—and
that would be the end of me."

It gave me a glimpse of the integrity of the man, someone
who would have to speak the truth as he saw it whatever the
cost. I've no doubt that is why he had such an influence on
Liddell, for integrity was the cornerstone of his character too.

When Liddell met him, Thomson was a minister of the
Church of Scotland pioneering new methods in evangelism.
One of his great concerns was for men, particularly young
men. He saw no reason why Christianity should be so ominously like a sinking ship—"women and children first." So he
ran meetings where the watchword was "muscular Christianity," or as some might call it "beef and Bible." Eric was an
obvious choice to Thomson for such a meeting. Would he
come and speak at a special "men only" event in Armadale,
Central Scotland?

Eric paused for a moment. Public speaking was not one of
his gifts, as he well knew. But inside himself he felt it was right

to accept. So April 6, 1923, saw him making his debut in public evangelism. He had never before spoken openly about his faith in Christ. But Eric had a great well of faith stored up in his heart—faith that spilled out for all to see. From now on he would be a marked man. A Christian he was before, without doubt; now he would be *known* as a Christian. His fame was growing, and it would be impossible for the public to disassociate Liddell the runner from Liddell the believer.

By all the rules Liddell should have been a nine-day wonder as a speaker. Once the novelty had worn off of the runner holding forth on his faith in public, the crowds should have dwindled, for in very truth he was no speaker. He was shy, hesitant, with no oratorical powers at all; yet the crowds came and he held them. There was something about his simple short sentences and his total lack of posturing that gripped an audience. There was no "ego trip"; he was *real.* People felt he truly cared, and that when he spoke about God, it was because he knew Him, and wanted others to know Him.

As Eric's speaking career got under way, so did the plans for the next Olympic games, now only a year away. What runners were doing in that 1923 season was going to be crucial for their Olympic selection in the next. Eric did not let his fans down. In London that summer he won the 220 yards without trouble, and the 100 yards in a British record which was to stand for 35 years. All this with a running style which appalled the purists. Head flung back, arms thrashing wildly, knees pumping exaggeratedly, he was like a man trying to beat a charging bull to the hedge. But it was the very moment that his head was flung back that his opponents came to know as the signal for "full steam ahead" when there would be no catching him. For Eric, it was sheer enjoyment. He hated to be beaten, as he confessed, but he seemed totally devoid of personal ambition. Chivalrous on the track, always making a point of shaking hands with an opponent before a race, the tantrums of some modern athletes would have been completely inexplicable to him, though, characteristically, he would probably have refused to criticize them, and insist on believing the best about their motives.

A week later he turned in a performance that should have warned those who the following year were to rate his chances nil in the 400 meters, for here in the English 440 yards, he not only won triumphantly, but did it after being knocked flying, picking himself up, and catching up the field from 20 yards behind.

He had a brilliant summer. Thus Eric's selection to run for Britain in Paris was a formality. But his running after he had been selected was certainly not. For of the two distances he was chosen to run in, 200 meters and 100 meters, the second race was scheduled to be run on a Sunday. And Eric said no!

Chariots of Fire had Eric make his dramatic discovery on the boat traveling to the games. In fact, he had the knowledge well beforehand, and the whole of Britain had plenty of time to realize that their star was not going to budge. It was a hurtful time for Liddell. He was accused of being a traitor, of letting the side down, of being stuck-up, narrow-minded, and who knows what else was said about him in the pub bars. On the other hand, there were those who admired his stand. Undoubtedly, those who knew him well could not doubt his sincerity.

The athletic authorities showed some understanding, and didn't take Eric's refusal as a snub. Otherwise, they would never have offered him the 400 meters. Anyway, he was too good an athlete to be kicking his heels on the sidelines when he could be running *something*. So Eric got down to the business of altering his training to fit the new distance. And those who watched him train were pleased with the way he developed. Could it be that this was his distance after all, the one for which he had real aptitude? The only trouble was, he hadn't really been tested against international opposition at this distance. He had a good win just before the Olympic games, but his time wasn't anything to write home about. Only the games themselves would show what he was really capable of.

Paris was hot that year—very hot. The Colombes Stadium sizzled like a frying pan. The long-distance races took their toll on the runners. But the crowd loved every minute of these games which saw the modern Olympics "come of age" to be the focus of world sporting attention it remains today.

Eric for his part was having a few qualms about his decision. His teammates still wanted him to run in the 100 meters. But he knew he had to stick to his guns, and pushed his doubts away. No one was more thrilled than he was to see Harold Abrahams win the 100 meters for Britain after all. (Eric had not seen the heats though; he was preaching in the Scots church in Paris.)

Eric himself had a medal in the 200 meters—the bronze. He then comfortably eased through his preliminary heat into the semifinals of the 400 meters. The semifinal itself he won also, though in a slower time than the other semifinal victor, Imbach of Switzerland, and his own teammate, Guy Butler, also in the other semifinal.

The stage was set for the race everyone had been waiting for. The morning's semifinals had produced the line-up that would bring the cream of 400 meters athletes together to decide the best of the excellent.

In the dressing room, Eric unfolded a small bit of paper. It had been handed to him by the team masseur. It read: *In the old book it says, '[He] that honors me I will honor.' Wishing you the best of success always."²*

Eric knew well the biblical reference: 1 Samuel 2:30. He smiled to himself. He believed that win or lose, God would be honored; but he was going to make as sure as lay within his considerable powers there would be a victory to celebrate that afternoon.

The broiling July sun was at its stupefying hottest as Eric walked out from the dressing room into the packed arena. His warm-up exercises made him sweat profusely, but there was no perspiration from nerves. His inward calm held good, even though the adrenalin was beginning to pump through his body as each minute to the start ticked away.

Suddenly, a noise fit to make the Eiffel Tower buckle shattered the buzz of trackside pep-talks, and Eric first grinned, then broke into a laugh, and waved to the kilted band-master of the Cameron Highlanders, who on an impulse had started his men into a bagpipe battle march. If that seemed a bit like unfair advantage, it only compensated for Eric's bad luck of the draw. He found himself in the outside lane, which meant that with the staggered start the track bend necessitated, he was in front, and would have no idea in the vital first yards where his opponents were.

Eric went to his fellow competitors and shook each one's hand. There was his teammate, Guy Butler; then he gripped the hands of the two Americans, Horatio Fitch and Conrad Taylor. He briefly but warmly exchanged clasps with the Swiss, Joseph Imbach, and finally the Canadian, David Johnson.

Brought to their marks, each runner crouched, muscles tensed, ready for the snap of released powder the gun would bring, straining their ears though the report would be heard over the whole stadium and beyond.

And there it was! Immediately, his reactions hair-sprung sensitive, Eric was away. It was as though instead of firing a blank, the starter's trigger had fired him. The crowd rose in astonishment at the pace the Scotsman set up. The keen spectators who carried their own stopwatches to meetings shook them in disbelief when they measured his 200 meters half-way time as 22.2 seconds. If their watches were right, he could never keep *that* up, surely. The rest of the runners were nowhere near him—a good three meters separated him from his nearest rival, teammate Butler. Yes, it was too good to last, and the British supporters, though cheering for all they were worth, saw the inevitable happen as Fitch's carefully paced race began to pay off, the American first passing Butler, and then stride by stride shrivelling the space to Liddell. But just as it seemed he must overtake, suddenly the front-runner threw his head back, thrashed his arms even more like a windmill, and pumped his knees as though he would hit his jutting chin. He was like a birdman taking off; and how he flew! He hit the tape in a blur of chaotic limbs, the crowd roaring itself hoarse. Fitch finished a good five meters behind, and Butler made a gallant third. It took a while for the crowd's excitement to subside before the loudspeaker announcement was made.

"The winner of the 400 meters is E.H. Liddell of Great Britain, and his time of 47.6 seconds is a new world record."

The Colombes Stadium re-erupted in a new burst of cheering and wild enthusiasm, which left no doubt in anyone's mind that this was the greatest and most popular victory of the whole Olympic games. Soon, Eric, his face trying to look appropriately solemn though inwardly he was laughing with happiness, stood on the winner's rostrum as "God Save the King" was played. After, with a quick wave to the still cheering crowd, he ran into the dressing room. The race was over. The Lord had honored him, as he had honored the Lord.

Back home, just before the Olympics, Eric had completed his Finals. The graduation ceremony to confer the degree he had gained gave his university and Edinburgh a golden opportunity to burst their buttons in pride, and they seized it with both hands. The journey to and from the McEwan Hall was almost a royal procession. Eric, modest and without an ounce of carnal pride, enjoyed every minute of it. In the hall, the cheering rolled in waves, bouncing off the elaborate paintings on the ceiling back down on to the heads of the students and their parents, then being sent up into the dome again in another cascade of sound.

The university authorities were wholly in the spirit of the occasion. The principal in his speech was justly cheered when he said, "Mr. Liddell, you have shown that none can pass you but the examiner."[3] He presented Eric with a Greek poem, specially written in his honor, which was probably lost on Eric who knew virtually no Greek at that time.

Later, at the graduation lunch, it was Eric's turn to make a speech. He put his philosophy of education in a simple direct way: "A man is composed of three parts; body, mind, and soul. It is only as you educate each part in harmony with the others that you will get the best and truest graduates from the university."[4]

Eric was a national hero, and for the next year he was *fêted,* he had countless invitations to speak and to preach, he even had a fan-club formed in his honor—and he still went on winning races, including once again beating his old Paris rival Fitch.

But Scotland knew that she shared the heart of her most famous son with another land across the sea—China. For a long time, Eric had been convinced that was where his future lay, and his purpose in taking his degree was so he could qualify as a teacher for the London Missionary Society. He did another year's course at the Scottish Congregational College, and by summer 1925, after spectacular valedictory meetings and a tumultuous farewell from Edinburgh railway station, he was in Tientsin in the land of his birth.

He arrived in troubled times. China was changing. There were warring factions, and there was plenty of anti-western feeling. The very school to which Eric had come to teach science and sports had its pupils on strike. However, a little over a quarter of the students turned up that first morning, and gradually all returned. Eric threw himself into the work with a will. He coached his students to be record-breakers themselves. He too ran in various events with continuing victories, and almost certainly could have taken part in the 1928 Olympics, but the selectors overlooked him. But that same year saw him in a unique athletic feat.

He was running in the 400 meters in Darien. As usual, he was first through the tape, but the cheering crowd became puzzled when he carried on running. He was on his way out through the race-track exit, picking up his travel-bag on the way, when suddenly he was stopped by the starting up of the British National Anthem, celebrating his victory. True patriot that he was he stood stock still to attention. Anthem over, he broke into a sprint again, only to skid to another halt when the "Marsellaise" began for the Frenchman who was second. Eric's chivalrous courtesy demanded that he stop again. The frustratingly long Gallic air over, he ran once more, straight through the open door of a waiting taxi. What the spectators had not known was that Eric had sportingly agreed to run in the last race knowing that his ship to take him to Manchuria was due to leave a mere 20 minutes after the event.

The taxi hammered its way along to the dock, and Eric sprang out to see the ship was at that moment cast off and gently nosing away. With hardly a moment's hesitation, Eric ran, threw his bag over the ships rails, and as the ship came back at him a little on a wave, he leapt. His gazellelike spring landed him safely on deck to recover his breath. Some were ready to say he cleared all of 15 feet of water. Whatever the distance, ever after he was given the name of the famous train: The Flying Scotsman.

Two years later, much to the surprise of his friends who thought he was a confirmed bachelor, he was engaged to Florence McKenzie, the daughter of Canadian missionaries, and 10 years younger than Eric. She accepted him without hesitation—he had won her by his humor and his honesty. He had the real "holiness" that isn't "goody-goody," but can afford a smile. But before they could marry, Florence had to complete her nurse's training in Canada, and it was also time for Eric's first furlough in Scotland, where he wanted to earn a theological degree and be ordained. So it was March 27, 1934, when the couple at last stood in front of the minister of the Union Church, Tientsin, and said "I will" into each other's eyes. Soon there were two daughters, and Eric proved himself a great family man. But as much as domestic bliss appealed to him, there came another challenge to surrender on the altar of God's call: and Eric answered yes.

There was a crying need for a pastor to go to work in the country area of Siaochang. It would involve months of separation, and would carry danger, because the area had been suffering the effects of war for some time. It was not without a great deal of prayer and heart searching that they both agreed that Eric should go, but once the decision was made, neither looked back. In 1937 he began his first work in village evangelism. But 1937 was also a first step in China for another party—and the intentions were not as honorable as Eric's. That year saw the first fateful shot fired that signalled the Japanese invasion of China. If Eric's missionary "patch" had known something of the suffering of war before from its own internal disputes, it was going to know something much more horrible now.

But despite the ominous times, the new country evangelist, called by his flock Li Mu Shi, got to work with a will and thoroughly enjoyed himself. His district was about 10,000 square miles, and he covered it mostly on foot or by bike. He had to visit churches, give advice to pastors, preach, teach, and all in the most primitive conditions. He loved it. His enjoyment was only marred by the times he would come across a burned-out village, or see dead bodies, the grisly calling cards of marauding soldiers. Civil war was giving way to the bigger war of the Japanese invasion. Eric's movements began to include bullet-dodging almost as routine. Weddings and baptisms were often conducted against a background noise of

gunfire and shell explosions, and there were ever more trage-
dies to cope with as cities were laid waste by the advancing
Japanese.

Once, on his way back to Siaochang, Eric was told of a
wounded man lying in a temple 20 miles away. One Chinese
man who owned a cart was willing to take the risk of going
with the missionary. They found the man lying in filthy conditions, and no one in the stricken city willing to take the poor
man into their homes for fear the Japanese would discover
them and make them pay the penalty. The enemy was only a
mile distant.

That night Eric wondered what to do if the Japanese
caught him helping their "enemy." He tossed and turned,
wrapped against the cold in his old sheepskin coat. He
reached out to his Chinese New Testament and flicked open
the covers. His eye fell on Luke 16, and as he read down the
Mandarin characters, his attention was grabbed by the tenth
verse: *"He that is faithful in that which is least is faithful also
in much: and he that is unjust in the least is unjust also in
much."* He had his answer. God, he felt, had given him a simple, straightforward instruction: *Be honest and straight.* Eric
slept sound and reassured.

Next morning, he saw God's delivering power, as he and
the carter entered a village, and saw the Japanese patrol go
right around it instead of through it.

Their mission to rescue the injured man almost completed, before they reached hospital, they were told of another
who had had a horrifying experience. Sentenced to be executed with five others, somehow or other the sword that had
slashed across his neck had failed to sever it, but he had been
left for dead. With a terrible, gaping wound, the victim was
miraculously still alive. Eric made a detour to pick him up,
and the little party made a perilous journey evading the Japanese troops and keeping out of sight of the circling planes.
They made it to the hospital, but sadly, their first casualty died.

The "executed" man, however, lived, became a Christian, and expressed his gratitude in a series of paintings that still survive.

The Japanese had by then taken over Tientsin, and the missionaries, including Eric's wife and family, were greatly restricted. At first, things were not too bad, and the family even managed to get in a furlough back home in Scotland and Canada. But things became darker and darker as the war progressed, and it became clear that while there was still a chance, Mrs. Liddell, now pregnant with her third daughter, should take the girls away to Canada. Eric was sad to see them go, but it never entered their heads they would not see each other again.

The move proved itself right when shortly after, all the foreign nationals were rounded up and sent to an internment camp at Weihsin. The motley group included business and administrative people, as well as missionaries. Eric was appointed "captain" of the missionaries group.

Though they were not considered "prisoners," their conditions were as close to prison camp conditions as they might be. Nearly 1,800 people lived in a compound of what had once been a school. The compound area measured roughly 200 by 150 yards. When they first got there, the place was a wreck, and the toilets were blocked and without running water. Gradually, some semblance of order was instituted, and Eric played his full part. His great sporting talents that had thrilled millions were now devoted to saving a handful of internees from getting dispirited, as he organized all sorts of games, using great ingenuity to improvise equipment: among his specialties was binding up hockey sticks with old sheets. But he was also moving around this conglomerate of people with a Christian presence that without preaching commended the Saviour to all. One internee, who later wrote of his experiences, came to disdain the missionaries generally, but made Eric his one exception, calling him "a saint."

As time wore on, and rumors filtered through that the war was turning against Japan, Eric found himself going through the (for him) strange experience of depression. He could not understand it. Admittedly, conditions were rough, enough to pull down the most resilient of people, but still it was not like him. He also began to experience headaches. But he shook it all off, and got on with his ceaseless work of organizing recreation, taking camp services, and writing his *Manual of Christian Discipleship.*

But then he was taken ill. At first, it wasn't thought it was anything more serious than flu worsened by the universal camp problem of malnutrition. But after an apparent partial recovery things took a dramatic turn for the worse. In hospital, the doctors puzzled over what was wrong. They did not find out before he went into his final convulsion, struggling out words to a fellow missionary, "It's complete *surrender.*" A last vomit, and he was gone.

The autopsy showed he had a massive brain tumor. Was it to that he had finally given in with his last word "surrender"? To all who knew him, the matter was never in doubt. His surrender at death was the surrender of his life: to Jesus Christ, his Lord and Saviour.

For further reading: *The Flying Scotsman* by Sally Magnusson (Quartet Books, London)

The Disciplines of the Christian Life by Eric Liddell (Abingdon Press)

Notes
1. Eric Liddell, *The Disciplines of the Christian Life* (Abingdon Press, 1985), p. 30.
2. Sally Magnusson, *The Flying Scotsman* (London: Quartet Books, 1981), p. 52.
3. Magnusson, *The Flying Scotsman*, pp. 71, 72.

10

Gladys Aylward

The tiny dark-haired girl could hardly believe what she was hearing. She sat on the hard wooden chair in front of the big desk looking in shocked dismay at the kindly, embarrassed face opposite, her interlocked fingers choking each other to death with the tension, her thin lips pushing hard against each other, disappointment creasing out from the corners of her mouth to every part of her face. Inwardly, a grief like that which accompanies the death of a loved one echoed around the shell of her numbed body. In a way there *had* been a death: the death of a dream.

"I . . . I . . . understand."

But she didn't really. She *couldn't* have gotten it wrong from God; she had been so sure.

The kind man who hated saying no to anyone, especially to someone as earnest and likeable as the distressed young lady before him, did his best to explain. He spread his upturned palms in an outward sweep over the papers spread in front of him.

"You see, Miss Aylward, the whole point of bringing you into our college for these three months was to test your call to China, and I'm afraid these exam results tell their own story. You're a wonderful personal worker, and you are a hard worker, but a scholar you'll never be."

He sighed sadly as he picked up one of the papers and shook his head slowly. Gladys remained silent, so he continued.

"Our China Inland Mission believes God will supply all our missionaries' needs, but we do believe as well that He will give the appropriate gifts for the job. You're 27—we've found that it's very, very difficult to learn Chinese at that age. You must reconcile yourself to the facts." Still Gladys looked at him dumbly, not daring herself to speak.

"Look," he said, speaking as brightly as he could, "I'm convinced the Lord has some work for you to do, but in *this* country. I tell you what, we have a couple just returned from China living in a house in Bristol. They need someone to keep house for them—I know you've done domestic service—why not go to them, for a while, at least?"

Poor Gladys! It was the last thing she wanted. And yet she knew it would be obstinate pride that would make her say no, so she mumbled something about thinking it over, and stumbled away from the painful interview to find herself a quiet corner where she could cry her heart out.

Friends she'd made in her exhilarating three months of training, sharing with her the joys of open-air witness, Bible study, and Christian fellowship, tried to console her, but the awful ache of disappointment just would not go away.

The whole crazy idea had started on a bus a few years

before (though it wasn't crazy to her). There she had been, a very ordinary person with a very ordinary job of parlormaid, reading a Christian newspaper about China and how it was so understaffed with missionaries. It was the kind of thing she could have read about a thousand times, and passed over without more than a flitted prayer to heaven for God to do something about it. But from that moment it was as though China became her life and breath. She talked about China, prayed about China, read all she could about China, until at last, the devastating realization imploded with a mighty bang: God wanted her to go to China. Never mind she was only an ordinary London working girl; never mind she had never passed an examination in her life, and had left school at 14; never mind she had a loving mom and dad, and younger sister and brother, Violet and Laurie, who would never understand and who would not want her to go. China it must be. It was His will, she was sure. In the nine years since she became a Christian on that wonderful night the young people of the chapel had whisked her into the special meeting, and she'd talked later to the minister's wife, she had learned how to listen to God through the Bible and the Holy Spirit in her heart. Confidently then she had carefully worked out her next steps, and they had led her to the door of the Women's Training Home of the CIM, with the motto she loved, "Have Faith in God."

But now the dream was in splinters around her feet and dissolving in her tears. She went to Bristol, and the grand old warriors gave her a motto for her Bible which encouraged her: "Be not afraid; remember the Lord."

Nevertheless, her disconsolate spirit was not satisfied, and so she had shortly gone on to Swansea, helping in a rescue work among "fallen women," with some hair-raising ventures into the streets and slums of the Welsh town that in those first years of the 1930s had plenty to shock a well-brought up daughter of a London postman and temperance worker. But

Gladys proved unshockable, and no job was too difficult for her initiative, or too dirty to be despised by her. She threw herself into the work with a tremendous zeal, and so salted everything with her Cockney wit that soon she was winning her way into many Welsh hearts. It looked as though the CIM's principal's words had come true: the Lord had work for her in this country.

But this country wasn't China. As the sunshine of God's word in the Bible dried out her tears, those dissolved splinters of her dream began to crystallize again, and the crystals grew, becoming more beautiful and compelling still, sparkling in that same sunshine of God's promises. Until at last the rays of hope bounced back to her too strong to be denied. "Be not afraid: remember the Lord." She *would* go to China yet!

She thought to herself, *I know it's God's will; through faith I can do anything. He can do anything. It just needs me to take Him at His word and all will be well.*

But she would need something else along with her faith, she realized: money. Well, she would earn it. She would go back to the only job she was able to do. Thus, not very long after, she was once more in London in one of the grand houses being shown up to the small servant's bedroom that was to be her base on the way to China. The moment should be consecrated to God, she felt. So she emptied her purse of her worldly wealth, two large old English pennies and one half penny, on top of her Bible, and she prayed.

"O God, here's my Bible! Here's my money! Here's me! Use me, God!"

That was as long as the prayer could be, because she was interrupted by another servant.

"Gladys! You're wanted downstairs."

Quickly smoothing her clothes straight and making sure her hair was in place, she scurried down to present herself to her new employer.

"Yes, ma'am?" she got out breathlessly.

"Miss Aylward, I hope you'll be happy with us. I want to settle up your expenses coming here. What was your bus fare?"

Gladys could hardly believer her ears. Apart from finding it a pleasant surprise that her new employer was so thoughtful as to reimburse her, her thumping heart rejoiced as she realized that the money she had so recently consecrated to God was suddenly going to be increased. A few minutes later she was bounding up the stairs with three shillings gripped tightly in her hand as though they were three jewels from the King of England's crown. At this rate she could be in China by next month!

Of course it wasn't quite like that. God was training her for one of the most remarkable missionary careers of all time and there were to be no short cuts. There never are with Him. But patiently, week by week from her job and extra hours work, the money grew.

She made serious inquiries at the travel office. The price of a boat to China horrified her. But then she found there was an overland route by train right across Europe and Asia—and it was half the fare.

"That's the one for me!" she declared excitedly. "I'll pay a deposit now, the rest weekly, then when I've got enough I'll have my ticket and go."

"Madam, you can't," said the clerk as patiently as he could. We don't take money on account, and anyway there's a war at the Manchurian border so we can't guarantee your arrival."

But the clerk discovered what many more, from missionaries to Mandarins, were to discover throughout Gladys' life: she had an iron determination and a sanctified cussedness that would never take no for an answer, especially if she believed God's will was at stake. And China was God's will for her all right. So the travel office clerk gave in, and the patient putting in of the pennies went on week by week.

Meanwhile, another little problem was solved; what she was going to do when she got there. She came to hear of a courageous retired Scottish missionary named Jeannie Lawson who had gotten fed-up with retirement and gone back at 73 to a remote mission station in northern China. She wanted someone to help her. Gladys lost no time! And soon there was Jeannie Lawson's reply in Gladys' shaking hand: get yourself to Tientsin, said Jeannie, and someone will bring you to me.

October 15, 1932, on Liverpool Street Station, Gladys' family gathered to see her off. Amid all the noise of engines belching excess steam, blowing whistles, and clanking rolling stock together, there was the lesser metallic noise of Glady's kettle, saucepan, and spirit kitchen stove knocking each other as she bundled into the compartment her suitcases, one full of clothes and the other full of food. The parting was keenly felt, but everyone was very brave and kept back the tears as best they could. But it would be 17 years before they would see each other again.

A 30-year-old woman traveling alone across Europe and Asia by train would have provided material for a gripping travel book in all normal times. And Gladys' record of her journey posted at various stops along the way would fill that role very well. But these were not normal times, and when she got to Russia and was approaching the Chinese border, she went from the realm of interesting travelogue to that of spine-chilling drama.

As the train had rumbled on across Siberia there had been a lot of comings and goings of soldiers. The man in the travel office had been right about the war. Gladys understood not a thing of what was going on, because of the language problem. So when the train groaned its way to a stop, with a great "phewwsss" of steam, she took not the slightest bit of notice of the train crew's attempt to get her to leave her seat. True, everyone else was getting out, but all she knew was the train had not reached where it was supposed to be going, so she stayed put. And when the train started again, she was content—until after a few miles it stopped in the middle of nowhere and all the lights went out. It was then she realized it was really going no further. It meant for her a long, long trudge for hour after hour along the track through the snow and biting cold to the last station. Perhaps it was the clattering of her saucepan and kettle still attached to her cases that kept at bay the wolf pack she could hear howling in the dark awesome forest as she stopped to have some food and some sleep part way.

Having made the station, her troubles were far from over. She had to face an interrogation from suspicious soldiers who could not make her out at all. They came to the conclusion that "missionary" on her passport meant "machinist." They had great need of machinists in the brave new post-Revolution Russia. She must stay. She frantically showed them her Bible, especially the pictures, to persuade them what she really was. At last they seemed to get some sense out of it, and it was somehow established that what she needed to do was to go to the great port of Vladivostock, get a ship to Japan, and from there, another ship to China. A couple of train rides and a thousand gesticulations later she was in Vladivostock. She found the Intourist hotel. She hoped it would not be long before the ship to Japan could be arranged. But there were more horrors. First, the clerk at the desk took her passport away. That was ominous. Next, the interpreter who had accompanied her to Vladivostock started arguing in an insistent way that she must stay; Russia needed machinists. He was getting quite angry. Then worst of all, the clerk came that night apparently to keep his promise of returning the passport.

But when she answered the expected knock, though the man was standing there with her passport, it was clear that was not all he had come for. He stood there, foot in door, tantalizingly waving the precious document just out of her reach, a lecherous leer on his face. He nodded his head in the direction of Gladys' bed. Her heart beat fast, and every woman's fear welled up almost to force a scream. But she didn't scream. Instead, she shouted with all the force she could muster from her five-foot-nothing frame, "God will protect me! God will protect me!"

And what happened next is only explicable by saying He did; the man looked as though he was going to fulfill his threat, but instead, he roared with laughter, left the passport, and went. Gladys, heart still thudding like a drum-roll, picked up the document and saw "missionary" had been changed to "machinist." She fled the hotel with the help of a girl who spoke a little English and had befriended her, and at last she was sailing away from a Russia for which she had understandably developed a profound dislike.

Jeannie Lawson was busy cleaning her dilapidated old house in Yangcheng when Gladys, clad now in Chinese clothes courtesy of missionaries met en route, arrived by mule, bumped and bruised from this last stage of her journey.

"Well, and who are you?" the old lady said.

It sounded rather unfriendly.

"I'm Gladys Aylward. I wrote to you from London."

"Well, you'd better come in."

The brusque welcome sounded more blunt than it really was. It was part of Jeannie's make-up, and the pioneering dare-all spirit that was hers. It needed a very special kind of person to operate an out-post of a virtually unknown mission with minimal financial support from "back home."

"Now, your name . . . . "

"Gladys Aylward," said the new girl, wondering just how forgetful the old lady would turn out to be.

"I know that, you cuckoo! I mean what are the *Chinese* going to call you? They'll never get their tongues round *that.* Let me see . . . how does Ai Weh Teh sound? It's close to

'Aylward' . . . . " She chuckled, "And it means 'The virtuous one.'"

"I don't know about being virtuous," said Gladys doubtfully, then decision swallowing doubt with bright certainty, "but Ai Weh Teh—I like it. That's who I am."

"Apart from your name, do you know any Chinese, Gladys? It's Mandarin here in these parts."

"None," said Gladys uncomfortably, realizing she would have to face up to the awkward truth of the principal's conclusion that to learn Chinese at 30 was beyond most—and she was no student.

"Well, you'd better learn some phrases to get by on before we do anything else," said the indomitable old lady. So she got down to the "impossible" task without more ado.

"This is what you say when you meet someone in the street, a polite greeting . . . . "

And Gladys made a delightful discovery as she mouthed her first Chinese words and tried them out with the Yang-cheng residents later. God *had* equipped her after all: she might not be much good with books, but she was a wonderful natural mimic, and the talent that before seemed only good for giving friends a good laugh became of enormous importance as she learned to cope with one of the world's most difficult spoken language, where pitch of voice can alter the whole meaning of a word.

But it wasn't easy. Nor was any part of settling into life in the old walled city, where time seemed to have stood still. Neither civilization nor attitudes had changed for centuries. One day she found, to her horror, she was witnessing the unceremonious public execution of a criminal. She gasped in utter shock at the flashing sword scything through the bared neck, and she ran blubbering into the house, to be told tartly by Jeannie that she would not be much use in spreading the gospel if she was going to react like that to every aspect of the culture she was now part of.

Also a shock, though not quite so traumatic, was to find she and Jeannie were regarded as "foreign devils." To be the targets for showers of mud was part of the missionaries' daily lot. It seemed that for all her years and experience, Jeannie hadn't yet found the key to unlock the hearts of the people of remote northern China. Until one day the veteran had an idea.

"Gladys!" she called excitedly, "I've got it! You know what this place used to be?"

"An inn," said Gladys. Jeannie had told her before how the ramshackle old place with its broken tiles and neglected courtyard had become hers at a tiny rent because it had the reputation of being haunted.

"Right!" Jeannie was waxing more and more enthusiastic. "And, an inn it shall be again. We'll open it to all the mule trains that pass through, give them good lodging for the night and tell them Bible stories for their evening's entertainment."

Gladys became as excited as Jeannie. There was a lot of work to do first, repairing the leaky roof, getting the courtyard straight, and making the rooms habitable, even for the undemanding Chinese standard of living. But at last it was ready, and all they needed was the customers. She soon discovered discreet invitations might be alright for the Ritz in London, but something altogether more bold was going to be needed here. So like a true innkeeper who had done it all her life, she planted herself in the path of the leading mule, grabbed the bridle with grim determination, and shouted, "No fleas! No lice! Good! Good! Come! Come!"

It worked. And so did the second part of the scheme, for Gladys found once more that God had in His own way equipped her. Her early ambition to be an actress found an outlet she had never dreamed of as Bible stories took wings under her imaginative telling. The characters of the ancient Israelites became living Chinese before her audience. They were enraptured.

Bit by bit, acceptance by the community became a fact,

and the people of Yangcheng came to love their "foreign devils." But the inn project had to come to an end when in a little
while Jeannie died. The little Christian community gathered
to pray over her coffin with its Chinese inscription.

Gladys was now a little stuck, for the regular income that
came via Jeannie was now dried up. But as she prayed help
came in a way that made her laugh and laugh. She was
appointed a government foot inspector.

For centuries, it was a Chinese custom to bind the feet of
young girls with tightly wound cloth bands to prevent their
growth. The tinier the feet, the more a girl was regarded. That
it meant they were also virtually crippled, unable to run without falling did not matter—it was even a bonus, for it meant
they could not run away from their husbands. The awful practice had been outlawed for 20 years, but in these remote
mountains, custom died hard. So it needed constant vigilance
from the ruler (the Mandarin) to make sure the law was not
broken. The problem was, he could hardly appoint a man to
this delicate task, and there was no suitable woman—so, why
not this strange English lady who was gaining such a reputation with her compassionate caring? Gladys was overjoyed. At
one stroke, she was going to have an income, and she was
going to get into hundreds of Chinese homes she would never
have had access to otherwise.

Her job increased her standing immensely. But she got
herself involved in something else that had an even more dramatic effect on the respect she commanded—a prison riot!

How or why the riot started she did not know, nor could
she understand how a woman foot inspector should be the
person to send for to crush it. But the official summons could
not be denied and there she was in the worried governor's
office.

"The men soldiers are frightened to go in," he mourned.
"The prisoners are killing each other. You must go in."

"Me?" screeched Gladys. "A missionary woman?"

"Yes, you. You always say your living God protects you."

Gladys swallowed hard. She felt her faith was on trial. She hesitated. But she knew she had no option.

"All right. Show me the way."

The heavy door was opened; she went through a dark tunnel, and then she found herself in the prison courtyard confronted by wounded and dying and men battling together in a chaotic tangle.

One convict had a chopper, red with blood, his intentions plainly to use it to wreak yet more havoc.

"Give me that chopper!" said the five-foot young woman to the ferocious man. Amazingly, he meekly handed it over. Everyone else froze. She lined them up, with them obeying her every word unquestioningly. Soon she was able to hand them over to the marveling governor. But if he thought his problems had all been solved, he was soon convinced otherwise. Gladys tore into him, criticizing the ghastly prison conditions, and the complete lack of any creative employment. The small woman had scored a remarkable triumph.

A while after the prison riot something happened that was to set the tone for a line of her ministry that was to be broad, thick, and unending until her death. A line of happiness and heartbreak, and which in a few years would lead her into one of the epic treks of history.

Walking out one day she came across a woman at the roadside, selling. But it wasn't food or trinkets she wanted Gladys to buy, but a girl. Gladys was horrified at this traffic in human flesh, and even more horrified to find there was nothing unlawful or unusual about it. It was the way of life. She bought the girl for ninepence—and from that time on as she grew up in Gladys' house that was her name, Ninepence. She was the first of child after child, baby after baby that Gladys was to look after throughout her life. Some children she would be asked to take in, others would simply be left on her door-step, without her ever knowing whose they were or from where they had come.

The pattern of Gladys' life now looked set, and though perhaps she never looked very far into the future, she could reasonably expect that the growth of the work would go on steadily, and she would live and die as an obscure missionary who had spent her life in a remote part of China. But ominous things were happening all over the world. Rumors began to fly about, even in these isolated parts. And as the '30s wore on, Gladys and her fellow citizens of Yangcheng began to hear distant noises of guns and planes. The rumors were true. The Japanese *were* in China. But surely, in this unimportant little place they would be secure?

But then came the awful day when the distant drone grew nearer and nearer, and then the deadly rain fell. Bomb after bomb fell on the tiny city, bringing horrific death and destruc-tion.

Numb with dismay, as the death-dealing planes flew on, Gladys came out of her bomb-damaged house and with one or two helpers, they did what they could for the wounded, and with that remarkable capacity to get people to jump to her commands, helped to restore order.

Now that the war had come to their peaceful home, deci-sions had to be made. The advancing troops who would fol-low in the wake of the planes could not be far away. Evacua-tion was essential. But where? And what about the children? With the bombing producing as one of its grisly fruits a crop of fresh orphans, the total number of children in Gladys' care was about a hundred. The best place to go seemed to be Sian, capital of Shansi, a trek westward inland of at least 250 miles! And there was the mighty Yellow River to cross—though the ferries should be able to cope with that. But what was the alternative? To wait for the Japanese, and whatever horrors they would inflict. If they stayed, Gladys herself would be in special danger, for the Japanese had put a price on her head, knowing that she had unashamedly spied for the nationalist Chinese. Gladys prayed. She was convinced God told her to go, so she got down to the preparations, and on a spring day in 1940 they left.

At first, it was like a Sunday School outing. They laughed and sang, and enjoyed their hike in the spring sunshine. But as the harsh realities set in after a day or two, it became a lot more difficult to keep up morale. Food was a continual problem. Once their supplies were gone, they had to eat what they could beg along the way, or gather from the fields. The little ones would sometimes want to be carried, the older ones needed to be constantly chided to stay in front where she could see them. The physical demands on all of them, including their dimunitive leader, were enormous. They sang choruses and hymns, all the time Gladys having to make sure the children never picked up from her any sense of anxiety, or worse, of despair. At all costs, for their sake as well as her own, she had to keep her faith bright, to trust with all her heart that the Lord who had been with her throughout would be with her still.

At last the broad muddy ribbon of the Yellow River came into view. It took ages to get to the bank, but the very sight of it renewed the excitement of the children. Yet as they got nearer, Gladys got ever more worried. Not a movement of any object did she see on that expanse of water at any time. When they arrived at the bank, her fears proved only too accurate. All ferries had been stopped. The boats had all been taken to the opposite side to deny them to the advancing Japanese. The ferry point was empty—a rough, wooden jetty making a promise it could no longer keep. Gladys could have cried enough tears to put the Yellow River into flood, but dare not for the children's sake.

Two nights and two days they stayed there, taking shelter in the deserted ferry-side town, occupied only by themselves and a handful of soldiers. The children occupied themselves as best they could, puzzling why they were not moving any more, but assuming that Ai Weh Teh knew best. Finally, one girl could bear it no longer.

"Why are we not crossing the river?"

"There are no boats," said Gladys, stating the obvious in the kind of quick, curt, way adults have when they don't want to be questioned any further.

"Then why don't you ask God to open the Yellow River like He opened the Red Sea in the Bible? You say nothing is impossible for Him."

Gladys gritted her teeth. She tried to explain that times were different. But it sounded very lame. In her heart she wasn't even convincing herself, for however different the times, God was the same.

"All right, we'll pray."

So there by the river she poured out her heart afresh to God, and pleaded that somehow, anyhow, He would get them across that river.

The answer was not immediate, but it was not long in coming. God did not provide a dry path through two walls of yellow water, but a serious, concerned nationalist officer. They needed to get across? They were too late for the ferries? He would see to it. He went down to the rickety jetty and gave a mighty whistle, carried on the breeze to the opposite bank. With a pair of binoculars he studied the far riverside for some sign of life. When at last some response came, a combination of whistles and gesticulations encouraged one small boat to put out and row with slow measured oar stroke towards them. It took many journeys before the hundred-strong party was over, but at last Gladys accompanied the last batch across, chirping "Hallelujah—thank you, Lord" and not caring who heard it.

Once the straggling, and by now ragged, group was over, Gladys got them all together and took stock. They still had a huge distance to travel. They were all undernourished, and she who had the incorrigible knack of being able to give her last crumb away to her worst enemy, let alone children she loved dearly, was probably more hungry than most. Nights of sleeping rough and days of foot-wearing marching had taken their toll. Yet they must go on. And so they began once again, weary mile after mile, the routine as before, singing their hymns, begging their food, and praying and trusting God to see them through. They managed to board a refugee train for part of the way, and after another period of marching the children had the great thrill of a ride on a coal train. Disembarked from that, a goodly layer of coal dust adding to all the other souvenirs of their march, and then at last, there it was: Sian.

Gladys went boldly up to the city gate, the children following like the dragon from their traditional New Year celebration. Gladys felt her heart sink as they approached. Though it was daytime, the gate was shut; something must be up. The keeper of the gate peered down at her from the wall top above her.

"You can't come in. We are full. No more refugees. Go away."

"But I have children here. We have come all the way from Yangcheng. You must let us in. We shall all die if we don't come in."

"No! No! No! Go away! We don't know you. You must go somewhere else. There is not enough food or room for us now. We cannot take any more."

Gladys sat down and cried, the tears cracking the caked dirt and coal dust on her face. She did not feel well, she was weak from exhaustion, and now this disappointment was too much. Some of the children wept with her.

"Can't we go in, Ai Weh Teh? Why are we still outside?"

There was one more hope. Before they had started out, the plan had been laid that once at Sian, and they had sorted themselves out, the older girls would go on to a refuge at

Fufeng, some way along. Well, they would *all* go there, and trust the Lord they would get in. They found there were refugee trains running that would transport them free of charge. They joined one, packed in the carriage tighter than a fat man in a thin man's pants. After a claustrophobic journey, they all were grateful to spill out as the train clanked and groaned to a stop at Fufeng. And yes, the city was open! Gladys' heart leaped. There was room for the children! They had made it!

Gladys made arrangements for her charges as best she could, and then typically, in this strange town, where she knew no one and no one knew her, she started right back on her job preaching the gospel. But she did not know how great a toll on her body and mind the awful strain of these months of treking had taken. In a very short time she collapsed under the strain.

Years later, her biographer, Alan Burgess, was talking to the Baptist Missionary Society doctor who, with others, brought her back to health. The doctor explained the package of illnesses he found her suffering from; he told of the weeks of delirium, the closeness of her brush with death. Burgess asked: "But Doctor—relapsing fever, typhus, a patch of pneumonia, malnutrition, exhaustion—how do you think, as a doctor, she managed to stay alive?"

And Dr. Stockley said quietly, "I can only presume that God had other work for her to do."[1]

The events bear out the truth of the doctor's remarks. Once recovered, she got back to work, then, at the war's end, was persuaded to return to Britain. While there, her way back to China was barred by the Communist takeover, but undeterred, she found plenty of work in Chinese churches in Britain. Then her life took a direction she had never dreamed of. An almost casual mention of her in a newspaper sent Alan Burgess after her to see if she might have a story. He was thrilled with what he found. It became a radio documentary, then a book, and then a film. To her immense surprise, she was a celebrity. Yet her heart was still with the Chinese people, and she returned to serve them, first in Hong Kong, and then in Taiwan (Formosa), the island to which the nationalist Chinese had fled.

Fame would not go away from her, though, and she found herself unexpectedly whisked back to London to be the subject of one of the most successful "This Is Your Life" programs Britain has ever seen. She captured a million new hearts. And while there, she lunched with the Queen and Prince Philip. The parlormaid who had served so many at table was waited on with all the stateliness becoming a royal guest.

Yet in spite of her celebrity status, still her love went to China and her people, and especially the children. When, in 1970, her Lord took her to Himself, there, in her little room in Taiwan, was another bed. On it the small, sleeping form of the latest, and sadly, the last, in that long, broad, procession of singing, laughing, Chinese boys and girls who had come to love Ai Weh Teh and loved her Saviour too.

For further reading: *The Small Woman* by Alan Burgess (Evans Bros., London)
Gladys Aylward: a London Sparrow by Phyllis Thompson (Word UK)

Note
1. Alan Burgess, *The Small Woman* (London: Evans Brothers, 1969), p. 227.

11

Athanasius

This lot won't listen to a thing I say. After all, I'm only the Roman Emperor."

Constantine groaned inwardly and glowered outwardly at the noisy arguing crowd that filled the spacious hall in the old palace in the Bythinian town of Nicea.

"I thought these Christians were supposed to love one another," he mused bitterly.

His eye roved over the agitated throng. As the very first Christian Emperor, following 250 years of persecution by his predecessors, Constantine felt he had a right to some sort of cooperation from these bishops and theologians of the church. In fact it was his cherished wish that the church would provide the string to tie together the shaky parcel of countries that formed the once impregnable Roman Empire. Instead, the string seemed only to be getting itself into knots.

Anyway, this council he had called, at great trouble and expense to himself, (300 bishops' traveling expenses did not come cheap, even to an emperor) had better get things sorted out once and for all. Trouble was, these religious people were all so passionate about what they believed. Constantine allowed a flickering regret to flare up in his mind for a moment; perhaps the old tolerant Roman way was best after all. Didn't matter what you believed as long as you acknowledged the emperor as divine too. But no, now *he*, the emperor, was a Christian too. The Jew, executed under the mighty rule of his predecessors, was his Lord now. But still, these Christian theologians . . . what a crew!

There was Eusebius of Nicomedia, a town quite close. Constantine liked him a lot. Someone he could confide in, he felt. But others thought Eusebius crafty. He was sitting not far from a scholarly looking man who always seemed to be writing. Another Eusebius. From Caesarea. Most confusing. Then there was Hossius, Bishop of Cordova in Spain. He had known suffering, as had a number present, from the great persecutions of the past. Some were minus eyes that had been gouged out, others had had leg sinews cut to prevent their running away. But that was past now—or so everyone hoped.

There was that fellow the fuss was all about standing over there, Arius. Good hand at writing jingles to put his teaching over, they said. He wasn't singing now, though. My, what a noise. His giant frame shaking with passion, veins on his neck bulging as he shouted for all he was worth, certainty in his eyes, thunder in his voice, and ruthlessness in the fist he smashed down on to his palm to make a point. Thankfully it was his last point (for the time being, at any rate) and he sat down quite suddenly.

"All right, Arius," said Constantine with relief, "thank you

very much. I didn't understand very much what you were saying, but I think it was something about Christ being created by
God, that there was a time when the Son was not."

Constantine shook his head slowly from side to side, not
even sure if he understood his own explanation of Arius' arguments. Constantine was a successful soldier who had won the
imperial crown by force of arms (plus, he believed, special
help from heaven). He was also a clever administrator who
had managed to re-unite the divided empire, astutely moving
the capital 900 miles eastward to the Bosphorus. But theologian or philosopher he most definitely was not.

"Alexander, your turn."

The aged archbishop from Alexandria in Egypt stood,
looking authoritative. He made a little deferential salute to
Constantine, with a little disdain. How could the emperor say
in his letter of invitation to the council that the cause of the
division between Arius and himself was "of truly insignificant
character and quite unworthy of such fierce contention"? The
very person and nature of the Lord Jesus Christ Himself was
at stake! Was the Saviour merely a creature like everyone else
seated in the great hall, or was he truly God come down to
earth? Alexander was determined to prove the second to be
the truth.

As Alexander delivered with passion and eloquence his
mighty arguments, Constantine's eye was drawn to the
auburn-haired young man sitting at Alexander's side. He
noticed the determined set of the jaw, the vigorous nodding
of the head in agreement. The young man was holding an
unrolled scroll, and seemed to be following Alexander's decla-
mation from it, stabbing here and there at a paragraph with
his finger. Then to his surprise the emperor saw Alexander
pick up the scroll and quote from it.

"No one else but the Saviour Himself, who in the beginning made everything out of nothing, could bring the cor-
rupted to incorruption; no one else but the Image of the

Father could recreate men in God's image; no one else but our Lord Jesus Christ, who is Life itself, could make the mortal immortal; no one else but the Word, who orders everything and is the true and only-begotten Son of the Father, could teach men about the Father and destroy idolatry."[1]

Constantine leaned across to Bishop Hossius, his chief advisor. "Who's that young man—and did he write that piece?"

"That's Alexander's assistant, a priest called Athanasius. People say he wrote that a few years ago. He's a very bright talent—very able. Alexander thinks the world of him."

Constantine nodded. He did not know at the time that the coming years were going to bring him quite a few headaches from coping with Athanasius. But for now, the pressing need was to get this council to come to a decision, a decision that, he hoped, once and for all would settle what the church believed about Jesus Christ, and a decision that would unite the church, and with it, the empire.

In the following days, the young man took more and more part in the debate. Constantine was surprised to see how small he was when he stood. But there was nothing small about his authoritative speech.

After much argument, the issue was resolved. A creed was produced that firmly came down on Alexander's and Athanasius' side:

> *"We believe . . . in one Lord Jesus Christ, the Son of God, the only-begotten of the Father, that is, of the substance of the Father, God from God, Light from Light, true God from true God, begotten not made, of one substance with the Father . . . . "*

Constantine was satisfied. With most of the work of the council done, he threw a great banquet to inaugurate the twentieth year of his imperial reign. All the bishops were invited.

Alexander and Athanasius were satisfied too. That phrase,

"of one substance" was one Greek word, *homoousion,* and for them the clincher. It meant that the opening statement of John's gospel, "In the beginning was the Word, and the Word was with God, and the Word was God," was being given its true and full weight: Jesus was ONE with God from the beginning. As they reclined on their couches, the royal feast piled high before them, they reflected on the time spent at the council. Not only had the creed stated clearly what they believed about Jesus Christ their Lord, but the council had anathematized, that is cursed, those who said, "there was a time when the Son of God was not," or that He was created. Arius, along with two others who would not sign the creed, was banished. To us, that seems harsh and unchristian. To them, it was logical and necessary.

Alexander was as pleased with the way his protegé had supported him, as he was with all the young man did. Born around A.D. 296 to a noble family, Athanasius had become deeply committed to Christ and the church at an early age, so much so that Alexander took the step of adopting him into his family. The two were like father and son. By the time of the Council of Nicea in A.D. 325, the archbishop's assistant had already made his mark with his formidable intellect. Already he had published weighty works of theology. Yes, mused Alexander, as he sipped his wine, this lad's going far.

Back in Alexandria in Egypt, the pair set to work in their routine tasks once more. It seemed the argument was over. Arius had been banished and was no longer in a position to disturb the churches under their care. Constantine was writing letters to reinforce the council's decisions, and bishops who had not been at Nicea were signifying their assent.

No one would have been more happy than Athanasius if the whole thing could have been laid to rest from then on. In spite of his rigid attitude to correct doctrine, he was a man who saw devotion as the very heart of Christianity. Indeed, the reason he felt so strongly about the divine nature of Christ was because of the worship that welled up in him towards the Saviour. He was a great admirer of those who showed the greatest love for Christ. His living hero was a hermit-monk, Anthony, who lived in the desert outside Alexandria. From him he learned how to discipline his body and mind in whole-hearted devotion to Christ and to the truth.

But events were not going to provide the desired quietness for tranquil devotion. Instead, he was to be tipped headlong into a whirlpool of almost constant activity, that would test his single-mindedness to the limit.

Rumblings of trouble began to echo down the east Mediterranean coast from the emperor. It seemed his resolution over the decrees of Nicea was wavering. He began to order the readmission of the Arians, demanding that Alexandria should take back Arius himself. Arius and his friends, especially Eusebius of Nicomedia who lived on the emperor's doorstep, were not inactive, and were vigorously campaigning, getting councils of bishops called who would support them, and generally doing all in their power to see their fortunes reversed.

Athanasius found that if there was to be a battle, then like it or not he would be in the forefront. Bishop Alexander lay dying. He called for his favorite. But the young priest was nowhere to be found. Another Athanasius came forward as the fading voice croaked the name, only to be ignored, while the bishop prophesied to the absent man, "You think to escape, but you cannot." On April 17, 328, Alexander died. For a time there was chaos. The old bishop had made it plain who his successor should be. The people of Alexandria, who had already come to love the youngster who was little in size but great in heart, clamoured for "the good, the pious, the ascetic Christian," who, they said, would be a "genuine Christian."

The bishops of Egypt and Libya would not agree for some time, perhaps because their sympathies were beginning to swing behind Arius, perhaps because of jealousy. But eventually, on June 8, with imperial authorization from Constantine himself, they consecrated Athanasius to the sacred office.

Immediately, Constantine ordered the new archbishop to take back Arius and his friends.

"If I learn that you have prevented any of them from returning to the church or have impeded their admission, I will immediately send someone to remove you by my authority and depose you from your offices."[2]

It was not that Constantine had changed his views on the person of Christ (he probably still did not understand the issues) but his great desire was for unity. He wanted peace in the church and in his realm. Discipline had been exercised; Arius had been dealt with. Now it was time to forgive and forget. Also, Eusebius of Nicomedia, Arius' strong supporter, was beginning to get an increasing influence over the emperor.

But Athanasius' theology was of tempered steel, and was honed to a sharp edge. The Scriptures (which he believed to be authoritative) were quite clear as far as he could see. There could be no smudging the clear lines it drew. He adamantly refused to take back the heretics, who disputed the teaching of the church. Athanasius held fast to the principle that truth does not change.

The "dirty tricks" department then came into full operation. There are some periods when things done in the name of Christ and his Church should make all Christians hang their heads in shame, and this is one such time. Eusebius of Nicomedia and Arius, along with other fellow travelers began making accusations to the emperor against Athansius to get him removed from his position as archbishop.

First, they claimed he had imposed taxes on Egypt to pay for vestments for the church at Alexandria. Fortunately, two of Athanasius' priests happened to be in court at the time and were able to refute the charge. Constantine wrote to Athanasius condemning his accusers, but commanded the archbishop to come to the palace at Nicomedia to answer for himself. When he got there, it was to face a new and more bizarre accusation. His opponents (at Eusebius' instigation) claimed that Athanasius' envoys had been responsible for a priest Athanasius regarded as a heretic being interrupted as he celebrated mass, throwing down the altar, burning the sacred books, and most blasphemous of all, breaking the wine chalice.

Athanasius' reply to the charge was comprehensively complete. There was no church at the place named; there was no chalice; the supposed priest was ill in bed on the day the outrage was supposed to have happened; and the renegade confessed to having been forced to accuse the archbishop.

One would have thought Athanasius' enemies would have licked their wounds and called it a day. Instead, they came back with a weirder plot still. They persuaded a heretical bishop called Arsenius to go into hiding, and then brought the accusation that the poor man had been murdered and dismembered by Athanasius for occult purposes. So serious was this accusation that a council was called to meet at Tyre in A.D. 335 to investigate it.

Prize Exhibit *A* was a human hand in a box, which when produced brought a cry of horror from all around. Little Athanasius looked unperturbed.

"Did any of you know Arsenius?" he asked.

"Yes, we knew him," many cried out.

He then fetched from the crowd a man with a shawl over his head, which was held down so no one could see his features. He bid the man lift his face, and looked around the council triumphantly.

"Is not this Arsenius?"

There was no doubting it was. Solid flesh-and-bone Arsenius.

Wise as a serpent, Athanasius some while before the council, had had a deacon go look for the "murdered" heretic, and, obviously someone who would have made his mark with the FBI in a later age, the clerical detective had discovered his quarry in a Nile-side monastery. To bring home the point, Athanasius had the resurrected Arsenius draw first one hand, and then the other from behind his cloak.

"I suppose," he said, with disdainful irony, "no one thinks that God has given to any man more hands than two?"

The muttering opponents put it all down to magic!

The beleagured archbishop may have triumphed in that one point, but as the council wore on with one accusation after another, it became plain that he was not going to walk from it without injury. It has to be admitted that behind all the mischievous plotting and evil lies there were some wounded spirits who had suffered at the wrong end of Athanasius' power-packed arguments which may have sometimes gone beyond words. To see the truth, especially divine truth, as clearly as Athanasius did, and to care about it so deeply, is to be driven to cut deep and straight furrows, whatever lies in the way. Athanasius decided not to wait for what seemed inevitable condemnation. He went down to the dockside at Tyre, boarded a ship for the Emperor's new capital of Constantinople (modern Instanbul), and there found Constantine as he was riding into the city. The emperor tried to ignore him, but small though he was, the persistent and fearless theologian planted himself firmly in the path of his Sovereign's horse. Grabbing the bridle, he looked Constantine directly in the eye.

"Either summon a lawful council or give me an opportunity to meet my accusers in your presence."

Constantine conceded the point, and immediately summoned the churchmen still at Tyre, which caused them much gnashing of teeth. The misguided Church leaders had been very busy. In their hated rival's absence they had buttoned things up nicely, having condemned Athanasius and pronounced Arius as the spokesman of truth. Some found the imperial summons ominous and fled, but the rest made their way to the capital. They knew they would need something a bit stronger if they were to bring about the archbishop's down-fall. So to Athanasius' total surprise, when at last they met in Constantine's presence, they made a completely new charge slyly designed to make the emperor feel threatened where it mattered most—in the stomach!

"Athanasius forbade the grain ships to sail from Alexandria to Constantinople," they said.

Athanasius looked at them with blank astonishment. "What! How could I, a private person, do anything of the kind?" he flared.

The wily Eusebius of Nicomedia, knowing he had his enemy off-guard, pounced. "In the Name of Our Lord," he said, "I say you did do it. You are rich and powerful and can do anything you want in your own city."

Athanasius flew into an indignant defense, but was cut short by the emperor. He was fed up. He did not really believe the charge, but he did want to be rid of this whole tiresome affair. If only he could get Athanasius out of the way, it would give him a bit of peace, and it might be a good thing for Athanasius too. Give him a chance to cool down perhaps.

"I find the charge proved. It is a capital offense, but in mercy my sentence is that you, Athanasius, shall be banished to Trèves in Belgica. I will instruct my son who rules the Western Empire from there to keep an eye on you."

Athanasius was defeated and left the emperor's presence a disconsolate man, mourning that he could not return to Alexandria to care for his beloved people. He made preparations for the long, long journey across the breadth of Europe. A few friends from Egypt accompanied him. It looked like it could be the end of Athanasius as a force for truth in the church.

In actual fact, things did not turn out so bad after all. He was received with kindness and honor by the emperor's son (also called Constantine) and was able to devote the next two and a half years to increasing his already enormous output of books. He kept in touch with Alexandria by letter (at some risk), and the Alexandrians did not forget or desert him. As far as they were concerned, he was their dearly-loved shepherd still. When Arius tried to go there, he got as warm a welcome as a cat in a dog pound and left with appropriate speed.

Following that, Arius signed a creed that satisfied the emperor of his orthodoxy, who then ordered the nearly 100-year-old (but far from senile) Bishop of Constantinople to receive him into the church. The old man prayed.

"Lord, take away my life—or else that of Arius."

As the exultant Arius drew near the forum, he was seized with violent pains and had to leave the party. He was discovered dead in the lavatory, which Athanasius heard with somewhat indecent delight.

Not long after, Emperor Constantine was taken ill. Just before he died, he laid aside his royal robes never to put them on again, and dressed instead in the white of a new student of the Christian faith, for though he had professed belief years before, he had never been admitted to the church fellowship. This was not unusual, for one of the strange beliefs commonly held in those days was that it was not possible to get forgiveness a second time after baptism, in which case to delay the rite until the last moment cut down the odds of any irredeemable slip. And an emperor had more chances of such a slip than most! The devious Eusebius of Nicomedia, who had such a hold over Constantine performed the baptism. Then on Pentecost Sunday, 337, the first Christian emperor died and was buried in his white robe in his new Church of the Apostles at Constantinople.

The Roman Empire was carved up between three sons. Constantine, Athanasius' great friend at Trèves, ruled part of the west as Constantine II; Constans ruled the other western half; Constantius ruled the east from his late father's throne. Things began well for Athanasius under the new emperor's rule. At Constantine II's insistence, he was restored to Alexandria. The people went wild with delight, and he was given the fourth-century equivalent of a ticker-tape parade. His faithful clergy called it the happiest day of their lives.

Unfortunately for Athanasius the situation rapidly changed for the worse. In 340, Constantine II was killed invading Constans' territory in Italy, and whatever moderating influence he had on his other brother who had jurisdiction over Alexandria was gone. Constantius turned out to be a thorough-going Arian. Eusebius was made Bishop of Constantinople, so was at the very heart of imperial power and had the ear of the new emperor whenever he wanted. The plotting and the accusing began all over again. Arius' death had done nothing to bring to an end the movement that bore his name. The Arians were strong, were flexing their muscles, and wanted Athanasius out! Their trump card was that Athanasius had been deposed years before by the Council of Tyre—which, of course, Athanasius had never accepted. Although the Egyptian church leaders backed Athanasius to the hilt, and though Julius, Bishop of Rome, tried to help, the power pushing evilly down from Constantinople was unstoppable. The Arians under Constantius' protection installed a bishop of their own, called Gregory, in a manner that made a nonsense of all the New Testament says about Christian leadership.

Gregory entered Alexandria with a large force of soldiers at the beginning of Lent, 340. Alexandria was in a fury, but the soldiers were not in the mood for opposition. A mob attached itself to the soldiers and mayhem broke loose. Churches were attacked, stores ransacked, books burned, altars profaned; there was drunkenness and sexual abuse.

Athanasius saw and heard all that was going on around him as he sheltered in his residence in the church of Theonas, and decided that to stop further outrages the only thing to do was to leave, which he did after hastily writing an official letter detailing the atrocities to let the world know what was going on. He was something of a journalist as well as a bishop.

Athanasius spent this second exile in Rome, where Julius

welcomed him with open arms. He became a sought-after teacher. People were captivated by his eloquence and his towering intellect. His ability to formulate what people believed and put it into words so that it made sense was unique. But what was liked most was that he was so obviously a genuinely pious man who loved Jesus. Single-minded to the point of ruthless he might be, but he was concerned not to win victories for his own glory, but for the Lord. He believed he had been saved by a Divine Christ, and no other kind of Christ, *could* have saved him. So the Saviour must be proclaimed in all His fullness with nothing subtracted. Not just Christ's glory, but man's salvation was at stake.

Athanasius further thrilled his hosts at Rome by his support of monasteries as retreats from the world where prayer and prayerful study could take place. Another subject of this book, Martin Luther, blessed the church by delivering it from the bondage of the cloistered life; but at this stage, with so much corruption in ordinary Christian circles, the saintly commitment of men like Anthony was a breath of pure air blowing across the tainted atmosphere, and those who were hungry for godliness responded joyously to it.

Meanwhile things were happening back east. The odious Eusebius died. Arians and anti-Arians each tried to put up their own new bishop and a riot saw 3,000 people killed. Constantius panicked and tried to get yet another council together to resolve all the differences. Fearing that Athanasius might even now come back, the Arians stirred up trouble at Alexandria. Some pro-Athanasians paid with their lives for their loyalty. Orders were given to the Alexandrian magistrates that Athanasius himself should be beheaded if he set foot in the Egyptian city. But the apparent change of heart of Constantius continued. He sent three letters begging the exile to return to Alexandria. As much as the Roman stay had been happy beyond telling, Athanasius knew he must obey, and it was what he wanted anyway.

He set foot on the familiar paving stones on October 21, 346. If his previous return from exile had been ecstatic, this exceeded it. The people streamed out in the thousands "like another Nile" stretching beyond the city. People burned incense all along the route. At night the city was as close to being floodlit as was possible in those ancient times before electricity, as blazing torches flaring towards heaven combined with thousands of oil lights that sent a flickering yellow glow of miniature flames dancing in celebration.

The excitement over, Athanasius settled down to what he hoped would be an unbroken period doing his real job of shepherding God's people. And so it seemed it would. A few years later Constans died, leaving Constantius as sole ruler. The emperor sent reassurance to the archbishop. "May Providence preserve you, beloved father, for many years!"

Athanasius received the greeting with gratitude.

"Let us pray for the good estate of the most religious Emperor Constantius Augustus" he announced in his church.

"O Christ, send Thy help to Constantius," the people responded.[3]

It might seem to a cynical observer too good to last. And it was. Constantius still had plenty of Arian advisors to poison his mind, and by now Athanasius' status was such that he must have seemed something of a threat to the emperor's supremacy. Whatever the reason, throwing overboard his profession of goodwill, Constantius embarked upon a dreadful program of harrassment and persecution of all those who held to the orthodox doctrine. Storm clouds gathered once again over Athanasius' head, and in 353 they broke. As before, there was the pattern of mounting charges, and a council being called to hear them. This time it was in the west, at Arles, where an Arian bishop presided, followed by another council at Milan. Athanasius was not there himself, but was represented by friends who defended him stoutly but unsuccessfully.

Envoys were sent to Alexandria to summon Athanasius to Milan. He refused. Meanwhile, troops were amassing around the city. At midnight on February 9, 356, Athanasius was in his church of Saint Theonas when the building was surrounded by 5,000 soldiers, plus the city mob, who were always good for a riot, whatever the cause. Suddenly the service was interrupted as the church was stormed. Doors began to break under the weight of the charging troops. Athanasius calmly turned to his assistant and instructed him to read Psalm 136, and the congregation to make the response, "for His mercy endureth forever." Twenty-six times Israel's triumphant ancient testimony rang out as splintering wood, crashing metal, and raucous shouts menaced the safety of the worshipers. As soon as the psalm ended, a hail of arrows rained down. Athanasius' loyal followers surrounded his bishop's throne in brave defiance as the troops advanced. Athanasius refused the urgent entreaties of his friends to leave.

"Not until the rest are safe," he protested.

But his life was too precious to his friends, and they unceremoniously wrenched him away to safety in the nick of time. It was one occasion when he could thank God he was small as he was successfully bundled out of the church into a side street, almost senseless from the rough handling. It was as well he did not witness the desecration of the church that followed his departure, nor the way his followers were beaten, kicked, and worse.

The Arians installed another bishop in Athanasius' place. The new bishop's name was George. Like Gregory, the usurper of 15 years before, he too was from Cappadocia. His ill-treatment of the followers of Athanasius was diabolical. The deposed archbishop could do little about it. Fleeing to his good friends, the monks and hermits who lived their lives of solitude in the desert outside of Alexandria, he became the "invisible bishop." He had all kinds of narrow escapes as he made stealthy visits to the city, always keeping one step ahead of his would-be captors, sometimes having to hide in a dry cistern. It seemed that the church was now totally lost to Christ-denying Arianism. It was *Athanasius contra mundum*—Athanasius against the world.

On his arrival among the cave-dwelling hermits, he was thrilled to be given the worn-out sheepskin coat of his great hero Saint Anthony, whose special request was that Athanasisus should have it.

For six years the archbishop moved among the desert dwellers. He spent much of the time writing, squatting down on a mat of palm leaves, a pile of papyrus by his side. One of the works he wrote was "Apology to Constantius" which he hoped one day to give to the emperor, and thus clear himself. However, he was never to have the chance to make the gift, for in November 361, Constantius died. Fighting a usurper, Julian, his half-cousin, he was struck down by a fever. It left the empire in pagan hands, for Julian had romantic notions of restoring the former Roman gods to glory. He was singularly unsuccessful, but he did some nasty damage on the way. But at first, the change of events worked in Athanasius' favor. He, along with the other exiled orthodox believers (for in spite of the *contra mundum* tag, there had always been those who had not bowed the knee to Baal) was permitted to return. This followed a terrible vengeance wreaked by the pagans on Bishop George whose atrocities they had hated as much as had the Athanasian Christians. However, the same pagans were not greatly pleased at having such a vigorous Christian as Athanasius back among them, so they complained to Julian. The pagan emperor listened, and without hesitation commanded him to leave Alexandria.

The faithful gathered around their leader with tears, as he faced exile for the fourth time. He cheered them up. "Be of good heart—it is but a cloud."

He got into a boat to take him up the Nile. But his enemies were not so willing to find him gone; they wanted him kept safely out of the way—or dead. Government agents jumped into another boat and gave chase. They strained their eyes to see any sign of him, as they headed up-river. They hailed a ship coming towards them.

"Ahoy there! Have you seen Archbiship Athanasius?"

"Yes—he is not far off!"

"Thanks"—and the men at the oars redoubled their stroke.

They passed the helpful man in the prow of the other ship, and he gave them a friendly wave. If only they had known . . . .

The wily archbishop, having been told he was pursued, had coolly turned his boat around in a bend of the river out of sight and sailed back past his foes.

Once more Athanasius' life consisted in trying to keep one step ahead of the law, but still he wrote and preached when and where he could. Often he would think martyrdom was near. But then in 363 came the news Julian was dead. Legend says that as he lay mortally wounded on the battle field he uttered the bitter cry "Galilean—thou has conquered." Whether or not this legend is true, for Athanasius, the cloud had passed.

Or had it? The new emperor, Jovian, was a rough and ready soldier who nevertheless received Athanasius cordially, and gave no encouragement to the Arians. But no sooner had Athanasius returned home from this meeting than he heard that Jovian had died in his bed, after reigning a mere eight months. The empire was once again shared out, this time between Valentinian in the west and Valens in the east. Under the influence of his wife, Valens was Arian, but for a while took no action. Then in 367 persecution began, and Athanasius found himself packing his bags once more. He managed to escape a few hours before the army came looking for him. They searched everywhere, inside, outside, even on the roof, but this expert in holy stealth evaded capture yet again. His hiding place this time was his father's tomb. There he holed out for four months. At the end of this time Valens had a change of heart and let Athanasius return. It was not worth the resentment it caused to have him away. So once more there was a rejoicing homecoming for the adventurous Archbishop.

The remaining years of his life were spent in relative peace. He still wrote, and he was still as vigorous as ever in defending the truth. Not only did he continue to argue passionately for the deity of the Lord Jesus Christ, but he was also the first to teach clearly the deity of the Holy Spirit; in fact it is to Athanasius more than to any other that we owe the doctrine of the trinity as Christians usually express it.

After such an action-packed life, with sudden and violent death a continual possibility, it's almost a surprise to find that he passed away peacefully in his bed. The date: May 2, 373. He was 77 years old. He had been a bishop for 45 years; 17 of those years had been spent in exile.

Was it all worth it? The answer is a resounding yes. If he had given up the struggle, Arianism would have triumphed. And if it had, such a debased view of Christ would have meant that in time Christianity itself would have disappeared from the scene, for the essential power would be missing.

Today we see the successors of Arians in such bodies as the Unitarian Church and the Jehovah's Witnesses, and in individual theologians who teach that Jesus was different to us only in degree. The stand Athanasius took for the unique Divine Sonship of Jesus is needed still.

For further reading: Any good history of the early church. Try to obtain from a library *Lives of the Fathers, Vol. 1* by F.W. Farrar (A & C Black, Edinburgh)

Notes
1. Tony Lane, *The Lion Concise Book of Christian Thought* (England: Lion Publishing, Tring, Herts, 1984), p. 31.
2. Robert M. Grant, *Christian Beginnings: Apocalypse to History* (London: Variorum Reprints, 1983), section XI, p. 11.
3. Bernard Reynolds, *Council of Nicea and Saint Athanasius* (London: National Society's Depository, 1911), p. 29.

12

C.S. Lewis

The hot, humid, New England night was sticky as a donut, and the stocky man seated in the glazed porch of his friend's Boston suburban home felt the iced tea warm through the glass from the heat of his hand. But he knew it was not the clammy air that was making him sweat so much as the turmoil going on inside him. For this was 1973, the year of the Watergate scandal that was to bring down the government of the most powerful nation in the world; and the man was Charles Colson, lawyer and personal confidant of the President himself. His previously unchallenged spiral to fame was about to run out of staircase, leaving nothing ahead but a sickening plunge to the bottom.

Yet the churning in his stomach wasn't entirely panic. There was a strange thrill of hope: there might be an answer. For his companion on the porch was Tom Phillips, a tall, gangling man with an enviable composure, and Tom was telling how his life had a little while before taken on new meaning when he had turned it over to Jesus Christ. Tom reached out to a table and took a slim paperback. "I suggest you take this with you and read it while you are on vacation."[1] he said.

Colson's eyes registered the title: *Mere Christianity* by C.S. Lewis. He then listened riveted while Phillips read a chapter. He had never heard the like of it before. He felt as if his past life, indeed his very soul, was being laid bare. The book went with him on his vacation. As he read, God changed his life. Charles Colson, soon to have his physical liberty taken away as the law took its unyielding course, nevertheless was to find *the* liberty that really matters, made free indeed by the Son of God. It was one of the most dramatic and significant conversions of this century. Yet at the time the slim volume was placed in Colson's hand, its contents had already been in print 30 years, and the author had been dead for 10. What kind of man was it who could write such long-lasting, relevant words?

"Mamy!"

When you're nine, and you've woken in the middle of the night with a skull-cracking headache, and a tooth that's playing kettle drums inside your gums, you yell. And you expect someone to come running to do something about it.

"Mamy! Mamy!" Young Clive Lewis yelled some more. But still no one came—at least, not to him. The strange thing was, there were all sorts of sounds coming from all over the house. People *were* around somewhere. Doors were banging, voices were raised, but for what seemed ages, no one came to the poor toothache sufferer. But then at last his father appeared in the doorway, and it was obvious from his haggard, grief-lined face that something more than Clive's toothache was filling his mind.

With tears and a breaking heart, Mr. Lewis senior, his lawyer's professional composure completely broken, haltingly explained as best he could to his son that Mamy was desperately ill with cancer.

Young Lewis had heard that praying in faith was the way to get God to do things, so he successfully worked up his faith to a good head of steam and confidently prayed for his mother to get better.

She died.

Lewis later maintained that this did not devastate him, but there can be little doubt that such an early experience of unanswered prayer must have contributed to the emergence of C.S. Lewis, atheist. For that is what the author of the powerful apology for Christianity that won over Colson was in his adolescence and early adulthood. Not that there had been a great deal to influence him towards a vibrant, personal faith in Christ anyway.

Born into a Belfast, Northern Ireland home in 1898, his parents were both intelligent, educated people who surrounded him with books. He had a brother, Warren, three years his senior, and the two boys were bonded into a closeness that was to last through their lives. In their early years before they were sent off to the British mainland to school, they were inseparable, and stimulated and fed each other's imagination as they created fabulous lands, peopled them, and wrote and drew the history and geography of their fictions.

In all of this, there was little place for God. The family maintained the formalities of a nominal church connection, but that was all. Whatever influence Mr. Lewis senior might have had was spoiled by an increasing distancing between him and his sons. It was not willful: it simply happened that two boys grieving over their mother whom they loved dearly found it next to impossible to relate adequately to their father. The net result was that their emotional and spiritual development went its own course, more or less unguided.

Not long after the tragic death of Mrs. Lewis the boys were sent to England to a most peculiar little school that could well have been in the novels of Charles Dickens. When he wrote his autobiography later, Lewis called it, with dark humor, "Belsen." Eventually, the cane-happy, sadistic man who ran it was to go mad, but before then, the two Lewis boys had mercifully been taken away.

Following a short spell at school in Ireland, the youthful Lewises were again sent to be educated in England, and this time the experiences were happier. By this time, the age difference meant that the two brothers were in different schools. But they were only a short distance apart in a beautiful English town, Malvern. Warren (or Warnie, as he was always called) was in Malvern College, while Clive (who preferred to be called Jack) was in a preparatory school linked to it, Cherbourg House.

Sadly, one effect of Cherbourg House was not so good. There was a matron, whose job it was to look after the boys' welfare and the smooth domestic running of the establishment. She was a perfect mother-substitute, and Jack adored her. Unfortunately, her rag-bag of odd beliefs, mixing up Theosophy, Rosicrucianism, and Spiritualism, was something she didn't mind tipping out in a heap and sharing with anyone who would listen. Jack first puzzled his way through the jumble, and then decided it was all rubbish and so sometime at Cherbourg House reached the point where he could deliberately and definitely pronounce himself an atheist. He was still only about 14 years old.

Such spiritual uplift as he felt he needed came from a strong, almost mystical affinity with the strange sagas and tales of the old Norse gods. He absorbed everything he could that spoke to him of "Northerness," whether it was Longfellow's poems (which had started him off) or Wagner's operas.

A couple of years later, he followed his brother to Malvern, having brilliantly won a classical scholarship. While there, he wrote a tragedy about the Norse gods, expressing his atheism in a paradoxical bitterness that was mad at God for not existing.

His stay at Malvern was brief. Unlike his brother, he hated the school, with its *Tom Brown's Schooldays* type approach. It had a structure where the older boys ruled the younger, often with great unfairness and bullying. He also hated the strong emphasis on games, for which he had no aptitude whatever. So it was that after much nagging to his father he was taken away from Malvern and sent to study with a private tutor in the Surrey countryside not far from London. This remarkable man's name was W.T. Kirkpatrick, known affectionately by Lewis' father as "the Great Knock." Under this eccentric man and his wife, Jack's intellectual capacity expanded to new dimensions to be filled with knowledge of all kinds. Jack's mind, always sharp, was honed to razor keenness. The Great Knock made Lewis forever declare war on sloppy thinking and inadequate reasoning—something that was to make Lewis later a formidable advocate of Christianity.

Lewis had a taste of what was to come the very first time he met the six-feet tall, shabbily dressed garden rake of a man. The teenage Lewis made polite conversation about how surprised he was at the scenery of Surrey, saying it was much wilder than he expected.

"Stop!" shouted Kirkpatrick. "What do you mean by wildness, and what grounds had you for not expecting it?"[2]

Sadly, the man who was to instill such precision of thought into Lewis was also to confirm him in his atheism. Nevertheless, these were peaceful years for Jack, as he stretched himself further and further academically. And it was not all spiritual loss.

One October evening he was on a railway station looking

at the bookstall. Just before the train came in he spied a book he had not come across before. He bought it just in time to put it into his pocket before he boarded. That night he read *Phantsastes, a Faerie Romance* by George Macdonald. To us, it sounds an odd volume to point a man to God, but as he read this unusual book by a Christian author, Lewis said he found his imagination "baptized," and he discovered a quality that had been missing in the other books he had read: holiness.

Nevertheless, Lewis was an atheist still, and he had a pressing problem on his mind: to get into Oxford University. There was no question of his brilliance in the classical subjects he wanted to study. To pass the entrance examinations in those was almost a foregone conclusion. But the problem was math: he had to take an exam in that as well, and he was hopeless! So Kirkpatrick worked on him for another year. If anyone could get him through it would be the Great Knock. But in fact no one could get him through. He failed.

But God overruled. It was now 1917, and World War I still raged. Because of the extraordinary disruption with many students and tutors called into military service, it was decided to admit Lewis anyway. And thus in April 1917 one of Oxford's most illustrious sons began his long association with the world's premier university. However, his initial stay was brief—just a few months. The same war that had opened the door for him to enter Oxford now took him away, for in a short time he too was in khaki, and by November 1917 was in the French trenches as Second Lieutenant Lewis, Somerset Light Infantry.

His military career was brief but eventful. It included contracting trench fever, capturing 60 Germans (a feat he always played down) and then getting wounded by a British shell that fell short. Consequently, he was back in a hospital in England before the war ended exactly one year after he joined it.

With health restored to his body and peace restored to his

country, Jack began his academic career in earnest at last. And what a career! Three degrees in a row, and all with first class honors! But brilliant or not, he found it no easy matter to get a job. In fact, he only took his last degree because there really didn't seem anything else to do. But no one can be a student forever, nor could he reasonably expect his father's generosity to go on stretching like a piece of everlasting elastic. The trouble was, there wasn't a great range of jobs Lewis *could* do. The Great Knock had written to his father years before with brutal frankness: "You may make a writer or a scholar of him, but you'll not make anything else. You may make up your mind to *that*."[3]

Fortunately for Lewis (and for his father) the chance to begin as both a writer and scholar was now his. He already had a book of poems in print while still a student, and his first post at Oxford was now offered—a year teaching philosophy at University College. That was followed by a fellowship at Magdalen College which was to occupy him until 1954.

He was now firmly on the road as a professional academic. But given his superb brilliance, why had there been such a stuttering start? It looked like the hand of God, for that final year of study, reading English not only gave him a second string to his bow, as he called it, but also brought him into contact with a new friend, Nevill Coghill, who steered him firmly (though perhaps unwittingly) in a Christian direction.

"I soon had the shock of discovering that he—clearly the most intelligent and best-informed man in that class-was a Christian and a thoroughgoing supernaturalist."[4]

Coghill was not the only influence that was turning the young atheist's mind in a different direction. There was also Owen Barfield, a man who was far from being an orthodox Christian. In fact, Lewis was to be fighting an intellectual "Great War" with him both before and after his own conversion, but Barfield succeeded in destroying forever what Jack called his "chronological snobbery." That is, just because an idea was old, it wasn't necessarily wrong; neither was a new idea necessarily right. Lewis's streams of books that flowed from him in later years defending and expounding traditional Christian truths bear witness how complete was the annihilation of "chronological snobbery."

Jack was beginning to realize a strange fact about his present life. That was for all his professed unbelief, the circle of friends he was drawn toward—and who were drawn toward him—were all Christian believers in some way or another, and all the books that were speaking most to him came from the pens of godly writers. Almost imperceptibly, he found himself in what was really a contradictory position. While still professing "there is no God" he was now talking about "the Absolute."

"I suspect there was some willful blindness," he commented later, realizing that what he wanted was to "get all the convenience of Theism without believing in God."[5]

As inconsistent as his position was, it was a landmark in the journey back to God.

"The great Angler played his fish and I never dreamed that the hook was in my tongue," he said. True enough—and the infinite patience of the Divine fisherman was perfectly willing to wait until the catch was ready to be landed once for all.

There is a romance about British double-decker buses that has even inspired poets. So the top of one trundling along an Oxford street seems as good a place as any for a divine encounter. As he was traveling on a perfectly ordinary journey, one he made often, Jack became aware he was holding something at bay.

"I felt myself being, there and then, given a free choice. I could open the door or keep it shut . . . . I chose to open."[6]

There were no blinding lights or thunderous voices. In fact, Lewis found the experience strangely unemotional. Nor was it an experience that suddenly rolled him off the assembly line as a perfect production-model Christian. He still could not even call God "God," though he had graduated as far as "Spirit"—albeit using the term in an impersonal way. However, he did begin to try to live his life in an ethical way as far as he understood it at that time. In so doing, he unwittingly was sealing off his escape-route, for he found God met him more than halfway, and brought him closer and closer.

"Really, a young atheist cannot guard his faith too carefully,"[7] was Jack's later wry comment.

Night after night in his room at Magdalen College he found that whenever his mind had a moment's freedom, it fastened on thoughts of God, and he felt the unrelenting approach of "Him whom I so earnestly desired not to meet." At last submission could no longer be denied.

"In the Trinity Term of 1929 I gave in, and admitted that God was God, and knelt and prayed; perhaps, that night, the most dejected and reluctant convert in all England."[8]

Even now Lewis could not describe himself as a Christian. He was a "Theist." He believed in God, a non-human God who had not been born in the flesh as far as he knew. Neither did he have any belief in a future life. How he did make these final important transition he was never quite sure. All he could ever recount afterwards was another journey two years later—not on a bus this time, but the back of his brother's motorcycle on a ride to Whipsnade Zoo one sunny morning.

"When we set out I did not believe that Jesus Christ is the Son of God, and when we reached the zoo I did."[9]

Writing his autobiography some time later, he finished the book with this conversion moment, but characteristically called that final chapter " The Beginning." That is a true statement about every conversion, of course, even that of the thief on the cross, who had only minutes to live when he found his salvation in a heart cry to the dying Jesus. But in Lewis's case, it was especially a beginning, for now a new career opened out to him alongside his academic one—that of a Christian apologist.

Christian apologists have a long and honored history throughout the Christian era. They are not people who are "apologetic" in the modern sense of being sorry, but their special gift is to present a robust, reasoned case for Christ and Christian belief, often in the face of ridicule and fierce opposition. In the early years many of them, such as Justin Martyr, paid for their boldness with their lives. Modern apologists may not have to face lions or go to the stake, but in a world that has generally thrown belief in God—particularly a supernatural God—overboard, stoutly to maintain and argue for belief in God and miracles takes a particular kind of courage. It does mean swimming against the intellectual stream.

Lewis was undoubtedly helped by some of the Christian friends he had. Not a man for large gatherings (he found it hard to settle into church life, especially as he was not over-fond of hymns or organs) he revelled in the company of a few companions of similar brain-power with whom he could debate and argue. So people like Dyson and Barfield were precious to him, and so too was J.R.R. Tolkien, a devout Catholic, who was to become famous later for his "Lord of the Rings" series of books.

It was not long before Lewis's first Christian essay was in the bookstores. Called *Pilgrim's Regress*, it was deliberately modelled on Bunyan's famous classic, and really told Jack's own story of how he became a Christian. Something of his cut-and-thrust approach to the enemies of Christian traditional truths came through in this early book as under the thinly-veiled figures of the allegory he slammed into both humanism and high-brow, arid, Christianity. In spite of all the obstacles, the hero, "John," eventually finds the true joy he has been seeking—and it is much nearer at hand than he ever imagined. "Mother Kirk" and his native country "Puritania" (the symbol for the church and the religion of his parents) had been both despised, but in the end brought him to the truth.

Some looked disdainfully at Lewis's return to "old time religion." The reviewer in the highly prestigious *Times Literary Supplement* declared it "the romanticism of homesickness for the past, not of adventure towards the future, a 'Regress' as he candidly avows."[10] The year of the book's publication, 1933, was a time when liberal ideas about Scripture and traditional Christian truths were largely to the fore. Any self-respecting intellectual who valued his standing among his peers could not afford to be seen embracing wholeheartedly and seriously the old ways. But Lewis was quite undismayed. He was taking his stand for a Christianity that was frankly supernatural and active. One of the figures he attacked in *Pilgrim's Regress* was a clergyman, Mr. Broad, who tells the hero there is a very great danger in making things "too definite." Conversion for Mr. Broad is far from being a necessity.

Though Jack Lewis's beliefs were old, his ways of expressing them certainly were not. In fact he was one of the most original Christian apologists there has ever been. This was eloquently demonstrated five years later when he published his first sci-fi novel, *Out of the Silent Planet,* which told the story of a trip to Mars by a Christian and two evil companions. Later years saw two more such tales told, each carrying a plain Christian message about sin, the effects of the fall, and man's willful ways.

When World War II gouged its awful wounds across Europe, Jack was not called up to fight a second time, though his older brother did serve in the forces again for a little while. Instead, he was given the task of lecturing to Britain's airmen about Christianity, and of broadcasting to the nation. This he did with spectacular success. His talks were published as *Broadcast Talks: Reprinted with Some Alterations from Two Series of Broadcast Talks* ("Right and Wrong: A Clue to the Meaning of the Universe" and "What Christians Believe" given in 1941 and 1942). With a title like that, you would hardly guess there was a paper shortage in Britain at the time! Mercifully, when Jack further revised them he also changed the title *Mere Christianity* —and 30 years later those two words began that life-changing experience for Charles Colson.

It's very tempting to think somewhat enviously of Lewis, the Oxford scholar with genteel friends and quiet surroundings, as having an easy Christian path—no bumps and scrapes from the rough rocks the devil puts in the path of ordinary work-a-day Christians contending with the rogues and wretches who try us to the limit of our patience and beyond. Actually, of course, the enemy of souls makes no distinction; he simply tailors his temptations to suit. Lewis was very conscious of the pitfalls that were there at a Christian's every step. And so he wrote about them with an originality that has never been surpassed. He imagined a senior devil writing to a junior who had the diabolical task of bringing a human to ruin. The book was called *The Screwtape Letters,* and was an immediate success. In fact it became the most successful of all his writings. Perhaps it gave people a smile in wartime, but the more likely reason for its runaway triumph is that people everywhere recognized just the kind of subtleties Satan tried on them. It is also true that Screwtape taught people a balanced attitude to the activities of God's enemy. Lewis said in his preface to the book, "There are two equal and opposite errors into which our race can fall about the devils. One is to disbelieve in their existence. The other is to believe and to feel an excessive and unhealthy interest in them."[11]

By the time the war was over, Jack's reputation as a Christian apologist was widespread. Though he traveled comparatively little, preferring long walking holidays in the English countryside to trips abroad, and revelled in the company of a small circle of friends (who used to meet weekly in a kind of literary club called "The Inklings") his books carried his fame far, not least to the United States, from where many would write to ask his advice. He always wrote back himself, often by return. In 1950, Lewis received a letter from a Mrs. Joy Gresham, who lived in New York. "Just another American fan," commented Jack's brother, Warnie, "with however the difference that she stood out from the rut by her amusing and well written letters."[12] Those letters were to be the beginning of the last great and most moving drama in Jack Lewis's life.

Before that was to develop, however, there was to be yet another amazingly original advance in the field of Christian communication, and the unlikely literary genre that was to be its vehicle was the children's story.

The origin of *The Lion, the Witch, and the Wardrobe* was a series of nightmares that involved lions. Lewis asked himself the question: "What might Christ be like if there really were a world like Narnia and he chose to be incarnate and die and rise again in that world as he actually has done in ours?"[13]

Jack read the first few pages out loud to Tolkien. (The Inklings often read their work to each other.) Surely the author of *The Hobbit* and *Lord of the Rings* would respond enthusiastically to something so akin in imaginative invention? He did not! In fact he told Jack he "disliked it intensely" and told another friend "It really won't do, you know."[14]

History, of course, has shown it would do, and do very well. The book became a series of seven that have delighted children and adults ever since. Children have followed the adventures of the four young heroes and the mighty Aslan with sheer innocent enjoyment, while preachers have discovered rich veins of golden Christian illustration that seem inexhaustible. The books remain models of how effortlessly a truth clothed in a strong story can make its point.

Two years after, *The Lion, the Witch, and the Wardrobe* was published, Joy Gresham came to England. Jack invited her to Oxford. Of Jewish extraction, she was a gifted writer who had become an atheist and a communist but had been helped to a Christian faith partly through Jack's writings. Her visit was a great success, and when the time came to go home, there was a mutual sadness at the parting. Not that anything remotely romantic had happened between the two at this time, Jack was apparently a confirmed bachelor who was somewhat thoughtless concerning other men's responsibilities to their wives when he wanted to keep them talking into late hours on some literary or theological subject. Joy was married. Her husband was an alcoholic who had prayed for and received help for his problem.

But on her return to America the marriage hit new trouble, and eventually it was mutually agreed to end it. Joy came back to England and settled in London with her two young sons. When Jack changed universities and began teaching at Cambridge in 1954 (though he still kept his house in Oxford) Joy helped him move. By 1955 she was living in Oxford not far from Lewis's home "The Kilns," to which he returned every weekend. She became a regular visitor.

In 1956 the British Home Office refused to renew Joy's permit to stay in Britain. Jack came up with an audacious scheme to help her. He would marry her. Not, as he saw it then, a *real* marriage but a civil ceremony, marriage in the eyes of the state that would give her the legal right to remain and to keep her boys in the British school in which they were so well settled. Joy continued to occupy her own house as "Mrs. Gresham." Jack believed all he had done was help a lady in distress.

It sounds an amazing arrangement, and some would wonder if it was a truly moral thing for a Christian to do. But as far as Lewis was concerned he had no qualms. He believed that true Christian marriage was something quite unique, and not to be confused with the mere legal linking of names that occurred when he and Joy stood before the civil registrar. He had no intention of consummating the union. For him, it was an act of Christian friendship.

However, things did not stand still—and neither did love. It was Lewis himself who published a Christian classic defining four kinds of love *(The Four Loves)*. It was a book out of his own life.

"No one can mark the exact moment at which friendship becomes love,"[15] he remarked to a friend. But though he could not name the moment, he came to realize it had happened to him. The middle-aged bachelor academic was deeply, deeply in love with Joy, and she with him.

He and Joy began to talk of moving in together, partly because Joy was having physical problems with what was believed to be rheumatism. Hospital tests then showed it was actually cancer of the bone. The prognosis was devastating. Her condition was terminal. The couple decided they must be married in the eyes of the church as well as the eyes of the state, and on March 21, 1957, a priest came into the hospital room and Jack and Joy were joined as man and wife in a Christian ceremony. Warnie found it heartrending as he saw Joy's eagerness to have the consolation of dying under the same roof as Jack.

Before the priest left the hospital room he did one more thing. He laid hands on Joy and prayed for her healing. It was courageous faith, for at the time one femur was eaten through and the cancer was spreading to other limbs. Yet from that time on a remarkable change began to occur. The cancer was not merely halted, but actual healing of cancer spots took place. Soon she was able to move about in an invalid chair, then actually to walk with the aid of a stick. The doctors used the word miracle.

For three years Jack and Joy had a joy in each other's company they had never dared to think possible. But in the fall of 1959 a check-up showed the cancer was breaking out again. There was to be no recovery this time, and after much pain and major surgery Joy died.

"I am at peace with God,"[16] she said to the chaplain just before.

An anonymous book appeared shortly afterwards, but few had doubts as to who the author was. It's title: *A Grief Observed*. It was probably the saddest volume Lewis ever wrote, but it helped him exorcise his pain.

By now, Jack himself was not in good health. He too had a bone disease, though not a malignant one. He had to wear a catheter and ruefully described himself as "a slippered pantaloon."[17] Yet still the writing went on.

In July 1963 he went into a coma and was expected to die. He did not welcome his recovery. He had seen an open door and had wanted to enter, he said. But he did not have long to wait.

Friday, November 22, Warnie brought his brother tea in the bedroom and Jack was alone. Pain arose inside and he struggled to get up and get to the end of the bed. He could go no further and slumped down with a crash. Hearing the thump, Warnie came rushing back. There was nothing he could do. C.S. Lewis was dead.

Four days later, on a cold frosty morning with wintry sun lighting up the yews with sparkling brilliance, the greatest Christian apologist of his age was laid to rest in the ancient churchyard of Headington Quarry parish church. One mourner noted, "One candle stood on the coffin. The flame burned steadily. Although out in the open air, it did not so much as flicker."[18]

It was a perfect picture of the Christian witness of the man.

For further reading: *Surprised by Joy* by C.S. Lewis (Collins)
Shadowlands by Brian Sibley (Hodder & Stoughton, London)
The many books of C.S. Lewis.

Notes

1. Charles Colson, *Born Again* (London: Hodder and Stoughton, 1976), p. 122.
2. C.S. Lewis, *Surprised by Joy* (London: Collins, 1959 [originally London: Geoffrey Bles, 1955]), p. 109.
3. Lewis, *Surprised by Joy,* p. 147.
4. Lewis, *Surprised by Joy,* p. 170.
5. Lewis, *Surprised by Joy,* p. 168.
6. Lewis, *Surprised by Joy,* p. 179.
7. Lewis, *Surprised by Joy,* p. 180.
8. Lewis, *Surprised by Joy,* p. 182.
9. Lewis, *Surprised by Joy,* p. 189.
10. Humphrey Carpenter, *The Inklings* (London: George Allen and Unwin, 1978), p. 50.
11. C.S. Lewis, *The Screwtape Letters* London: Collins Fontana Books, 1955), p. 9.
12. Carpenter, *The Inklings,* p. 233.
13. Carpenter, *The Inklings,* p. 223.
14. Carpenter, *The Inklings,* p. 223.
15. Carpenter, *The Inklings,* p. 239.
16. Carpenter, *The Inklings,* p. 250.
17. Carpenter, *The Inklings,* p. 250.
18. Carpenter, *The Inklings,* p. 251.